BY MICHAEL PARENTI

Blackshirts and Reds: Rational Fascism and the Overthrow of Communism (1997)

Dirty Truths (1996)

Against Empire (1995)

Democracy for the Few (1974, 1977, 1980, 1983, 1988, 1995)

Land of Idols: Political Mythology in America (1994)

Inventing Reality: The Politics of News Media (1986, 1993)

Make-Believe Media: The Politics of Entertainment (1992)

The Sword and the Dollar (1989)

Power and the Powerless (1978)

Ethnic and Political Attitudes (1975)

Trends and Tragedies in American Foreign Policy (1971)

The Anti-Communist Impulse (1969)

AMERICA
BESIEGED

MICHAEL PARENTI

CITY LIGHTS BOOKS
SAN FRANCISCO

Cover design: Small World Productions
Book design: Nancy J. Peters
Typography: Harvest Graphics

Cataloging-in-Publication Data

Parenti, Michael, 1933-
        America Besieged / by Michael Parenti.
            p.   cm.
        Includes index.
        ISBN 0-87286-388-7
        1. Elite (Social sciences) — United States.   2. United States
— Economic conditions — 1981- 3. United States — Social
conditions — 1980-   4. United States — Politics and
government — 1993-   5. Political participation — United
States.   I. Title.
    HN90.E4P37   1998
    306'.0973 — dc21   98-9487
                                                              CIP

City Lights Books are available to bookstores through our primary
distributor: Subterranean Company, P.O. Box 160, 265 S. 5th St.,
Monroe, OR 97456. 541-847-5274. Toll-free orders 800-274-7826.
FAX 541-847-6018. Our books are also available through library
jobbers and regional distributors. For personal orders and catalogs,
please write to City Lights Books, 261 Columbus Avenue,
San Francisco, CA 94133. Visit our Web site: www.citylights.com

CITY LIGHTS BOOKS are edited by Lawrence Ferlinghetti and
Nancy J. Peters and published at the City Lights Bookstore,
261 Columbus Avenue, San Francisco, CA 94133.

ACKNOWLEDGMENTS

My friend of many years, Kathleen Lipscomb, generously provided me with materials and suggestions that were essential in preparing several of the selections in this book. She also helped write an earlier version of the article on privatization. Jeff Crowl and Mark Mindful also contributed some helpful information. Charlotte Kates assisted in writing the selection on GATT and globalization. Jessica Luse contributed to the preparation of the manuscript, as did her father Robert Luse, whose technical expertise solved the problems of translating documents from one software system to another. Sally Soriano also rendered valuable aid, as did Nancy J. Peters, my editor and publisher at City Lights Books. To all these nice people, I offer my heartfelt thanks and appreciation.

CONTENTS

A DANGEROUS STATE

MANAGED MEDIA

CONCLUSION

PREFACE

In 1996, I did a weekly series of forty-five commentaries entitled "People's Radio." These were put up on satellite and played by some forty brave community and listener-supported stations throughout the United States and Canada and on Radio for Peace International, the world's only progressive, English-language shortwave station reaching audiences around the world. I was pleased to discover that "People's Radio" won an enthusiastic reception. Among the commonly heard listener responses were "Why haven't I heard this before?" and "Why don't the people in public life talk about these things?"

Many listeners requested transcripts of the talks. But time and money constraints made it impossible to distribute transcripts — and eventually made it too difficult to continue the broadcasts themselves.

Now in this book I have reproduced the heart of the commentaries, many of them revised and expanded, so that they might be accessible to interested persons. Also included are several selections I never had a chance to broadcast.

Radio commentaries usually deal with the events of the day: the president's spending proposal before Congress, his pending trip to China, his chances for reelection, or a congressional leader's waning popularity, the likelihood of a tax cut, predictions about the stock market's performance, and an array of other such topics that are the stuff of punditry—all treated in the major media from a limited center-right ideological perspective and in a superficial manner that soon leaves them outdated.

In contrast, the selections in this book focus on the underlying and enduring forces in modern U.S. society; they provide a useful critical framework for understanding what passes for "the news." That's why I believe they have retained their relevance, and that's why they continue to be played in their original form on a number of radio stations.

Now in revised and I think improved condition, they are offered here to those who still find nourishment in books, even books that say forbidden things.

STRANGE POLITICS

AMERICA BESIEGED

The various commentaries in this book are linked by a common critical perspective, one that is not directed against our nation but against those who are mistreating our nation. Those of us who love our country — not as an ideological abstraction but as a place where millions of decent people live out their lives — are not willing to see it go down the drain just so that the select few can accumulate more and more wealth and power for themselves. The plutocrats' goal is to secure and expand their already enormous share of the world's wealth and stamp out alternative ways of organizing society at home and abroad, regardless of the costs to the rest of us.

For years we were told to be alert to the Red Menace. Lurid images were painted of communists infiltrating our national institutions. Never was the possibility considered that the communists were doing no such thing, that they played a leading role in the struggle for industrial unionism, civil rights, and peace, and that in fact they were loyal Americans, dedicated to the needs of common people and opposed to the free-market abuses of the capitalist system.

Now that the supposed Red Menace has receded, the established powers conjure new demons: Islamic terrorists, homegrown terrorists, "eco-terrorists," "troublesome" ethnic minorities, immigrants, subverters of family values, feminists, gays, welfare mothers, politically correct liberals, "cultural elites," "secular humanists," and the government itself; that is, those government agencies that might try to regulate business—with an eye to protecting the public interest. To this list may be added anyone else who proves inconvenient to moneyed interests or who can serve as a scapegoat against whom the public might direct its real but misplaced grievances.

To clamor about these various "threats," as right-wingers do, is to overlook the real threat posed by the corporate class itself, its enormous power in making things happen the way it wants. Today, rich multinational corporations, assisted by their ideological acolytes in and out of government, take in billions of dollars in direct and indirect public subsidies. The practice of feeding public money to private business interests has become so widespread at the federal, state, and local levels as to have earned the sobriquet, "corporate welfare."

The big corporations batten off a massive profit-driven military budget. As rich creditors who hold the enormous notes on the national debt, they pocket billions of taxpayer dollars. They themselves enjoy billions in tax write-offs and tax credits. They support those who attempt to undermine public services. They push for passage of laws that expand the repressive powers of the national security state, and international agreements that undermine democratic sovereignty and give free rein to monopoly capital. They work to destroy social reform movements at home and abroad, to strip away environmental protections, to marginalize progressive leaders, and ever more tightly limit political discourse in major media that are neither free nor independent.

So one is forced to conclude that we are indeed a nation besieged, not from without but from within, subverted not from below but from above. The moneyed class exercises a near monopoly influence over our political life, over the economy, the state, and the media. Some Americans are astonished to hear of it. Others have had their suspicions, though they may not be quite sure how it all adds up. This book invites the reader to stop blaming the powerless and the poor and, in that good old American phrase, start "following the money." Let's keep our eye on who has too much of the real power in this country. That is the first and most important step toward lifting the siege and bringing democracy back to life.

THE EVASION OF POLITICS

Politics is something more than what politicians do when they run for office. Politics is concerned with the struggles that shape social relations within societies and affairs between nations. The taxes and prices we pay and the jobs available to us, the chances that we will live in peace or perish in war, the costs of education and the availability of scholarships, the safety of the airliner or highway we travel on, the quality of the food we eat and the air we breathe, the availability of affordable housing and medical care, the legal protections against racial and sexual discrimination — all the things that directly affect the quality of our lives are influenced in some measure by politics. The right to travel to other countries; to hear and voice dissenting opinions in the media, the workplace, or the classroom; to have some protective control over our work situation and environment; to avoid having our labor underpaid and exploited; to live with some measure of security and opportunity at a decent standard of living; to be protected from crime in the suites as well as crime in the streets—these are important political rights, at least as important as listening to campaign speeches and voting.

To say you are not interested in politics, then, is like saying you are not interested in your own well-being. Of course, just about everyone is interested in their own well-being. But many people do not see how political forces act directly upon their personal lives.

They are not entirely to blame for this. Much of popular culture in present-day America is organized so as to distract us from thinking too much about the larger realities that act upon us. There is the celebrity world, the doings of movie stars and pop singers, and the endless sporting events. There are the mind-shrinking idiocies of commercial television—everything from sitcoms and shoot-'em-ups to daytime quiz shows, soap operas, and music videos. There are the fads and enthusiasms, the cults and sects, the joggers and bikers, the diets and cures, the fashions and life styles; and we must not forget the televangelists who focus people's attention on personal pieties and protective deities, promising that God will help them financially if they help the televangelists financially.

There are parts of popular culture we look down upon and wish people would forsake, and parts we secretly enjoy ourselves. Most of us indulge ourselves in such distractions from time to time. After all, it is easier to be entertained than informed, although it is seldom more interesting. But the fluff and puffery of entertainment culture is so omnipresent that it can easily crowd out more urgent things.

In economics, Gresham's Law says that bad currency has a tendency to drive good currency out of circulation. There seems to be a Gresham's Law in popular culture: the more sensationalized and hyperbolic images and events crowd out the more substantive ones. By constantly appealing to the lowest common denominator, a sensationalized popular culture lowers the common denominator still further. Public tastes become still more attuned to the big hype, the trashy, flashy, wildly violent, instantly stimulating, and desperately superficial offerings.

Even many of the issues that supposedly deal directly with political life are devoid of any intelligent discussion of the political realities that actually weigh upon us—which helps explain why we do not find them very compelling. Much of what is called "politics" in America focuses on the pursuit of elective office. Twenty-two months before the November presidential elections, the news media are filled with stories about who might run for the Democratic and Republican nominations (with not a word about third parties, except perhaps conservative ones). The main focus throughout the ensuing months is not on the issues but on the horse race: Who is running? Who's ahead? Who dropped out? Who has the voter appeal? Who won the nomination? Who will win the election? No wonder opinion studies indicate that the public has felt turned off by the endless politicking, the mudslinging, and the enormous sums of money expended during campaigns.

The formal education most Americans get does little to rectify matters. Usually they are fed a pabulum version of American history and American society that dares not delve in any critical way into the exploitation that has been imposed upon labor, the oppression of minorities and women, the abuses perpetrated by corporate America at home and abroad, and the repression of dissent at home and of democratic forces in other countries by U.S. leaders. Many Americans know very little about other countries and the destruction wrought by U.S. ruling elites abroad.

Most Americans are taught next to nothing about the social forces that shape history and society. They lack a coherent picture of what has happened in the world, in the distant and even recent past. This leads to some odd confusions. To cite just one small but significant instance: a recent poll discovered that something like 25 percent of our compatriots thought we had fought against both Nazi Germany and the Soviet Union in World War II. (In case you are of that 25 percent: the Soviets fought on our side against Germany, inflicting and sustaining the major portion of the casualties.)

Americans are taught that we have a free and open society as befits a self-governing people. Unlike the poor souls in "totalitarian" countries, we supposedly are involved in and are informed and critical about political affairs. Soviet dissident Alex Amerisov, who chose to live in the United States, when questioned about this some years ago, came to a contrary conclusion. What struck Amerisov was how markedly apolitical Americans were as compared to Soviet citizens, how Americans almost never concerned themselves with political issues, with the important events that bear upon their lives and communities, at least not in any sophisticated and informed manner. In contrast, in the Soviet Union, according to Amerisov, people were always discussing issues and registering their complaints and ideas.

With today's capitalist restoration in the former Soviet Union, however, the level of political apathy and cynicism now resembles that of our own country. The point is that Americans have been made notably apolitical by the popular culture and social forces that act upon them. American political socialization is largely an apolitical one and this itself is a significant political fact.

In addition, Americans face the time-consuming need to earn enough money in order to survive in an expensive, cutthroat, work-driven society. Many people are too busy making a living to be able to make history; that is, to have the time and resources to act politically. They are compelled to pursue their immediate interests in ways that often violate or leave them unable to defend their overriding long-term interests. Furthermore, the political structure is so organized around big-money campaigns and mass media exposure as to leave them feeling excluded from realistic participation.

Many Americans shy away from politics because they feel defeated before they start. They may give every appearance of being apathetic, but often apathy is just a cover for a sense of powerlessness. Feeling overwhelmed by events, many people experience a sense of futility about political life. So they avoid getting involved. Given a political culture that encourages passivity, superficiality, and individual spectatorship—rather than collective action—it is small wonder that people do not see how they can change things for the better. Having no easy access to the resources of power, they feel powerless.

Luckily for the democracy, not everyone feels that way. Millions of Americans do try to make a difference. They try to educate themselves and others. They organize and agitate, protest and demonstrate. They speak out and fight back against things they do not like, in the workplace, in their communities, in the nation. And often they do make a difference. In many instances, their need to make a living *does* dovetail with their ability to make history, as when they organize at the workplace and struggle for job protections, better occupational standards, and better wages. In the course of those struggles they often have to confront the powers that would keep democracy from developing.

In sum, politics is a subject we cannot afford to ignore. By "politics," I mean the struggles around just about every life-and-death issue there is, encompassing so much more than the electoral hoopla to which the term is usually applied. Politics will wreak its effects upon us whether we like it or not. By educating ourselves to how political realities affect our lives, we become more effective citizens, better able to defend our own interests and those of our community, our nation, and our planet. The study of politics, then, is itself a political act of the utmost importance.

THE PRESIDENT AS CORPORATE SALESMAN

The president of the United States, we learn in school, plays many roles: chief executive, commander-in-chief, "chief legislator," head of state, and party leader. Seldom mentioned is his role as guardian and representative of corporate America.

Presidents do their share to indoctrinate the public into the corporate business ideology. Every modern president has had occasion to praise the "free-market system" and denounce collectivist alternatives. Presidents are solid believers in the business ideology of a market-driven economy. They boost the virtues of self-reliant competition and private initiative, virtues that exist more clearly in their minds than in the actual practices of the business community.

The president is the top salesman of the system, conjuring up reassuring images about the state of the union. Presidents would have us believe that our social problems and economic difficulties can be solved with enough "vigor" and "resolve," or by "toughing it out," or through "self-reliance" or a "spiritual revival," as various White House occupants from Kennedy to Clinton have put it.

"America is number one," proclaimed President Nixon, while millions of his unemployed compatriots were feeling less than that. "America is standing tall. America is the greatest," exulted President Reagan to a nation with sixty million citizens living below or close to the poverty level, a record trade deficit, and a runaway national debt. Prosperity, our presidents tell us, is here or not far off—but so are the nation's many wild-eyed enemies, be they communists, revolutionaries, or terrorists. There is no shortage of adversaries abroad supposedly waiting to pounce upon the United States, held back only by huge military appropriations, CIA covert actions, and a strong internal security system. Presidents usually downplay crises relating to the economy and emphasize the ones needed to justify U.S. interventionism abroad, huge military budgets, and curbs on political dissent.

Whether Democrat or Republican, liberal or conservative, the president tends to treat capitalist interests as synonymous with the nation's well-being. Presidents greet the accumulation of wealth as a manifestation of a healthy national economy, regardless of how that wealth is distributed or applied. America will achieve new heights spurred on "by freedom and the profit motive,"

President Reagan announced. "This is a free-enterprise country," said President Clinton, who added: "I want to create more millionaires in my presidency than Bush and Quayle did." Presidents will describe the overseas investments of giant corporations as "U.S. interests" abroad, to be defended at all costs — or certainly at great cost to the U.S. populace. In fact, a president's primary commitment abroad is not to democracy as such but to the global "free market."

In the past century, almost all Republican and Democratic presidential candidates have been millionaires either at the time they first campaigned for the office or by the time they departed from it. In addition, presidents have drawn their top advisers and administrators primarily from industry and banking and have relied heavily on the judgments of corporate leaders.

A president's life style does not make it any easier for him to develop an acute awareness of the travails endured by ordinary working people. He lives like an opulent potentate in a rent-free, 132-room mansion known as the White House, set on an 18-acre estate, with a domestic staff of about one hundred, including six butlers and five full-time florists, a well-stocked wine cellar, tennis courts, a private movie room, a gymnasium, a bowling alley, and a heated outdoor swimming pool. The president has the free services of a private physician, a dozen chauffeured limousines, numerous helicopters and jets, including Air Force One. He also has access to the imperial luxuries of Camp David and other country retreats, free vacations, a huge expense allowance—and for the few things he must pay for—a generous annual salary.

Journalists and political scientists have described the presidency as a "man-killing job." Yet presidents take more vacations and live far better and longer than the average American male. After leaving office they continue to feed from the public trough. Four ex-presidents (Ford, Carter, Reagan, and Bush) are multimillionaires, yet each receives from $500,000 to $700,000 in annual pensions, office space, staff, and travel expenses, along with full-time Secret Service protection costing millions of dollars a year. Our tax dollars at work.

Presidents and presidential candidates regularly evade federal limits on campaign spending through a loophole that allows big contributors to give what is called "soft money" directly to state political parties. Big contributors may disclaim any intention of trying to buy influence, but if it should happen that after the election they find themselves or their corporations burdened by a problem, they see no reason why they shouldn't be allowed to exercise their rights like other citizens and ask their elected representative, who in this case happens to be their friend, the president of the United States, for a little help.

For their part, presidents seem as capable of trading favors for campaign money as any influence-peddling, special-interest politician—only on a grander scale. The Nixon administration helped settle a multibillion-dollar suit against ITT and received a $400,000 donation from that corporation. Reagan pushed through the deregulation of oil and gasoline prices and received huge contributions from the oil companies. President Bush's "Team 100" consisted of 249 wealthy financiers and corporate CEOs who put up at least $100,000 each to help elect Bush in 1988. In return, they enjoyed White House handouts, special dispensations on regulatory and legal matters, and appointments to choice ambassadorships. And President Clinton adhered faithfully to the practice of selling favors for funds to affluent clientele, using White House facilities to solicit campaign money, taking contributions from foreign donors—which is prohibited by U.S. law—and from other fat-cat contributors who were compensated with special favors.

It is said that the greatness of the presidential office lends greatness to its occupant, so that even persons of mediocre endowment grow from handling presidential responsibilities and powers. Closer examination reveals that presidents have been just as readily corrupted as ennobled by high office, inclined toward self-righteous assertion, compelled to demonstrate their military "toughness" against weaker nations, and not above operating in unlawful ways. Thus, long before Bill Clinton thought of doing it, at least six other presidents employed illegal FBI wiretaps to gather incriminating information on rival political figures.

The White House tapes, which recorded the private Oval office conversations of President Nixon, showed him to be a petty, vindictive, bigoted man who manifested a shallowness of spirit and mind that the majestic office could cloak but not transform. President Reagan repeatedly fabricated stories and anecdotes about nonexistent events. The Iran-contra affair revealed him to be a deceptive manipulator who pretended to support one policy while pursuing another and who felt himself to be unaccountable to Congress and the Constitution.

To get to the top of the political power heap the president must present himself as a "man of the people" while quietly serving those who control the wealth and power of the country in ways that are pleasing to them. If presidents tend to speak one way and act another, it is due less to some inborn flaw shared by the various personalities who occupy the office than to the nature of the office itself. Like any officeholder, the president plays a dual role in that he must satisfy the major interests of corporate America and high finance and at the same time make a show of serving the public.

Although some presidents may try, they discover they cannot belong to both the big corporations and the people. The success any group enjoys in winning presidential intercession has less to do with the justice of its cause than with the place it occupies within the class structure. Presidents usually decide in favor of big industry and finance and against light industry and small business, in favor of corporate shareholders and against workers.

On infrequent occasions the president may oppose the interests of individual companies. Hence, he might do battle with an industry like steel, as did Kennedy, to hold prices down in order to ease the inflationary pressure on other producer interests. When engaged in such conflicts the president takes on an appearance of opposing the special interests on behalf of the common interest. In fact, he might better be described as protecting the common interest of the special interests. This role is not sufficiently appreciated by the business community, who will attack a president for even the most minimal regulations he might feel contrained to impose.

On even more infrequent occasions when an issue is given some honest exposure in the media and public sentiment is mobilized, the president might decide on behalf of the public interest, as when Clinton backed his Food and Drug commissioner against the tobacco companies regarding the marketing of nicotine. Still for all the publicity, not all that much has been done to stop that industry from marketing its addictive and injurious products to publics at home and abroad.

Generally, as the most powerful officeholder in the land, the president is more readily available to the most powerful interests in the land and rather inaccessible to us lesser mortals—unless we organize and raise more hell. The best thing we can do is never romanticize the individuals who occupy the highest office or, for that matter, any office.

OUR LEADERS
DON'T KNOW BEST

Through the centuries antidemocratic theorists have
argued that leaders should form their own decisions and
not be responsive to popular demands; public affairs
should be left in the hands of knowledgeable decision
makers, who supposedly know things the rest of us do
not know. Political leaders are the first to encourage
uncritical faith in themselves. I recall how Vice President
Spiro Agnew admonished people for demanding "too
much" democratic participation in public affairs. Just as
patients must rely on their physician's expertise for medical care, so citizens must depend on their leaders, the
experts in statecraft. Ordinary people can no more expect
to make decisions about policy than about medical treatment, he maintained.

Not long after this utterance, Agnew was indicted
for using the influence of his office to perform special
favors for special friends. In return, these friends — who

doubtless were appreciative of his expertise in state-craft—regularly delivered large sums of cash to him at the vice president's residence.

In 1991, Polish president Lech Walesa, dedicated to privatizing his country's economy, demanded that the democratically elected parliament suspend its powers and make way for rule by presidential edict. This was necessary in order to deliver the blessings of the free market upon a population that was becoming resistant to subjecting themselves to the continued "shock therapy" of unemployment, inflation, and the loss of human services and benefits. Responding to this popular sentiment, parliament resisted some of Walesa's draconian measures.

For Walesa, democracy had become a troublesome barrier to the transition to capitalism and had to be stuffed back into the bottle. He resorted to the same kind of anti-democratic elitist analogy as Agnew, arguing that a bus must be driven by the driver and not by the passengers, who might all try to grab the wheel at once and who would succeed only in plowing the vehicle into a tree.

Such arguments against democracy are endless in the history of political theory, going as far back as ancient Greece. They are often framed as arguments by analogy and, as such, they make overextended comparisons between things that are really quite different. The relationship of democratic citizen to officeholder is not the same as the relationship of patient to doctor or passenger to bus driver. But if one really wanted to argue the analogy, one could draw different conclusions from the ones proffered by Agnew and Walesa.

Thus, contrary to Agnew, patients should show no more unquestioning trust toward doctors than citizens toward officials. Patients should ask about the purpose of specific medical procedures, get second opinions, and make the final decision on whether to submit to a particular treatment. Too many doctors are trained to act with the same arrogance as Agnew's public official, not listening to what patients have learned from their experiences with their illness.

So with Walesa's analogy of the bus: while passengers should not grab the wheel, they certainly have a right to know where they are being taken, by whom, over what course, at what speed, and with what degree of competence and safety. And if they don't like how or where the bus is being driven, they usually can vote with their feet and get off at the next stop—which is something we cannot easily do living in a polity.

No matter how appealing the analogy may be, one is still comparing situations that are at best only roughly parallel in form while vastly different in content. No analogy about doctor-patient or passenger–bus driver relations can settle the original question regarding the appropriate role of democratic input in public affairs.

The notion that people should trust their leaders has

led to many unfortunate outcomes. History is full of examples of monarchs, dictators, prime ministers, popes, and presidents who were not deserving of the slightest trust, who pursued policies that violated the interests of their people at every turn. During the Vietnam War, I heard someone remark that the president must know things we do not and therefore we must put our trust in him and follow his lead. During the 1991 war waged by the United States against Iraq, I heard a student say the same thing: we had to "trust" the president and "have faith in him."

Such expressions of faith should discomfort every democrat. Faith is something we might better reserve for a deity. Trust, as exists between close friends and loved ones, is the one thing we could do without in regard to our leaders. Especially during times of crisis, such as war, we hear that we must have faith in our leaders, for they are the ones who will see us through. What is overlooked is that they are likely the ones who created the crisis and should be held accountable for their actions.

It is the essence of democracy that we *not* trust and *not* have faith in our leaders. Democracy is a system built on *dis*trust. That is why — when a close approximation of it works — we get real debate, investigation, exposure, and accountability. At the heart of all procedural democracy is the idea that we must watch leaders closely, question them sharply, demand to see the documents, look for differing explanations, and pursue open debate about policies, before, during, and after elections.

Being a leader is no guarantee of special wisdom or virtue — as Agnew, Walesa, and so many other leaders have thoroughly demonstrated. If one reads the minutes of presidential meetings or the correspondence between top decision makers or listens to a president or cabinet member at a press conference or reads the memoirs of erstwhile leaders, one is impressed by how *un*expert the policymakers sound, how their thinking seems free of particular enlightenment or insight. One is struck by the self-serving manipulation, the fabricated justifications, inconsistencies, evasions, and downright lies, and the contrived and often superficial arguments that are conjured up to justify domestic and foreign policies that serve elite moneyed interests rather than popular interests, and thus have no real democratic justification.

One comes away with a better understanding of why leaders so often insist on working secretly, without having to give an account of their actions. They do not want us to see what they really are about.

To those who counsel "trust" and "faith," I would ask: Who among our ruling agencies should we trust? Should it be the CIA, which carries out violent covert actions against rebellious peoples abroad, and which has a long record of colluding with conspirators, assassins, and drug traffickers? Should we place our faith in the

FBI, with its COINTELPRO, a systematic campaign to infiltrate and subvert democratic groups with provocateurs and undercover agents, and with its murderous raid against private citizens in Waco, Texas? Should we trust the president, who said that NAFTA and GATT would create a more prosperous and equitable life for folks at home and abroad, and that ending aid to families with dependent children would be good for those families? Or should we trust the Republicans in Congress who seek to dismantle every environmental regulation that is still on the books and want to roll back Social Security and every other governmental human service that reaches common people, while expanding the huge services and handouts that go to rich corporations?

I would not trust any of them. I would trust only a vigilant, informed, distrustful citizenry: we, the people.

REPUBLICRATS AND DEMOPUBLICANS

It is not quite accurate to characterize the two major political parties, the Republicans and Democrats, as Tweedle-Dee and Tweedle-Dum. Were they exactly alike in image and posture, they would have even more difficulty than they do in maintaining the appearances of choice. The question is not, Are there differences between the two parties? but, Do the differences make a difference? On most fundamental economic issues, the similarities between them loom so large as to obscure the differences.

With the exception of a small group of Democratic progressives in the House of Representatives (numbering about fifty) and a few progressives in the Senate, both political parties in Congress are committed to the preservation of an untrammeled giant corporate economy, huge military budgets, and the funneling of public monies through private conduits in order to bolster business profits. With relatively few exceptions, both are committed to the use of repression against opponents of the big-business structure, the defense of the multinational corporate empire, armed intervention against social revolutionary or nationalist elements abroad, and the transfer of sovereign power to international business oligarchs under NAFTA and GATT—all at great cost to the life chances of people at home and abroad.

The similarities between the parties do not prevent them from competing vigorously for the prizes of office, expending huge sums in the doing—just as the similarities between Coca-Cola and Pepsi-Cola do not keep them from strenuous competition, and the similarities between the Gambino gang and the Gallo gang did not keep them from bloody turf fights.

As with other commodities, the merchants of the political system have preferred to limit their competition to techniques of packaging and brand image. With campaign buttons, bumper stickers, and television and radio spots, with every gimmick devoid of meaningful content, the candidate sells his image as he would a soap product to a public conditioned to such bombardments. As someone once said, "You can't fool all the people all the time. But if you fool them once, it's good for four years."

Whatever their differences, the two major political parties collude in maintaining their monopoly over electoral politics, and discourage the growth of progressive third parties. All fifty states have laws that are written and enforced by Democratic and Republican officials, regulating and frequently thwarting third-party access to the ballot. Such laws require vast numbers of signatures for third-party or independent candidates just to get on the ballot.

Minor parties also face limitations on where and when petitions may be circulated, who may circulate them, and who may sign. In some states, the time allotted to collect signatures has been cut to one week, making it virtually an impossible task. In West Virginia, Arizona, Nebraska, New York, and Texas, you cannot vote in a major party primary if you sign the petition of an independent or third-party candidate to help them get on the ballot.

Filing fees also discriminate against minor party candidates. In Florida, an independent or third-party presidential candidate must submit 167,000 valid signatures, and pay ten cents for each one, which is a minimum filing fee of $16,700 just to get on the ballot. In Louisiana, an independent candidate must pay a $5,000 filing fee just to try to get on the ballot — in other words, just to engage in the process of collecting signatures. The Democrats and Republicans face no such requirements, having fashioned the laws to suit their two-party monopoly.

Restrictive ballot requirements supposedly are necessary to screen out frivolous and kooky candidates. But who decides who is frivolous and kooky? And what is so dangerous about such candidates that the electorate must be protected from them by all-knowing, major party officials? Who appointed the Democrats and Republicans as our protectors to determine which candidates are acceptable? In fact, the few states that allow easy access to the ballot, such as Iowa and New Hampshire, where only 1,000 signatures are needed and plenty of time is allowed to collect them, have suffered no invasion of frivolous or kooky candidates. If you want kooks, try the Republican-dominated 105th Congress.

Federal law provides millions of dollars in public funds to the major parties to finance their national conventions, their primaries, and presidential campaigns, even though they are *private* parties. But public money goes to third-party candidates only after an election, and only if they can gather 5 percent of the vote, which, in a national election, is about 4 million votes. In other words, the smaller parties cannot get the money unless they get 5 percent of the vote. But they are not likely to get 5 percent unless they get the money that can buy them national media exposure.

The Federal Election Commission, designed by law to have three Republican and three Democratic commissioners, spends most of its time investigating and filing suits against smaller parties and independent candidates. Thus, two private political parties have been endowed with public authority to regulate and harass other parties. We Americans would balk at seeing any particular religious denomination designated the state religion, to be favored by law over all other religions. Indeed, the First Amendment of the Constitution explicitly forbids governmental establishment of any religion. Yet we have accepted laws that, in effect, make the Democrats and Republicans the official state parties, a rigged two-party monopoly, and this at a time when they are less popular than ever.

The very system of representation discriminates against third parties. The single-member-district, winner-take-all plurality elections used throughout most of the United States, tend to magnify the strength of major parties and the weakness of smaller parties. Winner-take-all means the party that polls a plurality, be it 40, 50, or 60 percent, wins 100 percent of a district's representation with the election of its candidate. The smaller parties, regardless of their vote, receive zero representation, thus suffering a higher percentage of wasted or unrepresented votes. The minor parties invariably win a lower percentage of seats, if any, than their actual percentage of votes.

An example of how the minority party is deprived of representation is provided in the 1994 U.S. House elections in Iowa. The Democrats won 42 percent of the votes but won none of the seats, thereby wasting all their votes. In the 1992 U.S. House elections in Washington state,

Republicans received 42 percent of the votes but wasted most of them, winning only one of nine seats. The same kind of distortions occur in Canada, Great Britain, and the few other countries that use winner-take-all, single-member districts. In the 1997 Canadian national election, the Liberal Party won only a 38.4 percent plurality of the vote but received a majority of the parliamentary seats. In Britain, the Conservative party of Margaret Thatcher and John Major kept getting around 60 percent of the seats in parliament for almost two decades without ever having received more than 44 percent of the popular vote. Meanwhile a smaller third party in Britain would receive around 20 to 25 percent of the vote, without ever winning more than 3 or 4 percent of the seats.

What we need is proportional representation, or "P.R." as it is sometimes called. Under P.R. a party that gets 40 percent of the vote gets 40 percent of the seats, a party that gets 15 percent at the polls gets 15 percent of the seats, and so on. Proportional representation is the most popular voting system in the world. New Zealand has just adopted it. Some form of P.R. is used throughout Europe, Scandinavia, and elsewhere, producing governments that are consistently more representative and responsive than winner-take-all systems. In the United States, a few local governments and school districts have used P.R., and a few more are in the process of adopting it.

The winner-take-all system eventually deprives the

minority parties of voters since not many citizens wish to waste their votes on a minor party that seems incapable of achieving a legislative presence. Sometimes it does not even seem worth the effort to vote for one of the two *major* parties in districts where the other major party so predominates and will be winning the sole representation. But if we had P.R., every vote would be given some representation, and people would be more likely to vote. Indeed, in countries that have P.R., there is a broader choice of parties, a higher rate of participation, and greater representation of various groups.

Then there is the problem of voting fraud. The computer-based punch-card systems used nowadays are at least as susceptible to error, accident, and fraud as paper ballots and voting machines. Investigations reveal a high instance of tabulation errors and easy opportunities to distort counts. In an election in St. Louis, ballots in working-class, African American wards were more than three times less likely to be counted than those in white wards. Punch-card voting irregularities have been found in many states.

To maintain the status quo, authorities will resort to more coercive measures than vote fixing, if need be. Almost every radical group that has ever managed to gain some grassroots strength has become the object of official violence. The case of the American Socialist party is instructive. By 1918, the Socialist party held

1,200 offices in twenty-four states. But soon after, the Socialists suffered the combined attacks of federal, state, and local authorities. Their headquarters in numerous cities were sacked by police. Their funds were confiscated, their leaders jailed, their newspapers denied mailing privileges. After a few years of this treatment, the party was finished as a political force. While confining themselves to legal, peaceful forms of political competition, the Socialists discovered that their opponents were burdened by no similar compunctions. The guiding principle of ruling elites is: when change threatens to rule, then the rules are changed.

For most voters, a political campaign has little reality apart from its media visibility. Since the media do not cover a third party's campaign, most people remain unaware of its existence. During presidential campaigns, the television networks give the Democratic and Republican candidates prime-time coverage every evening, while minor party candidates receive but a few minutes of coverage, if that, in their entire campaign— unless the minor candidates are conservatives like George Wallace or Ross Perot.

If the two major parties are so good, why do they need such a rigged system to maintain their hegemony? Those of us dedicated to democracy can begin by pushing for reform in our electoral system, including laws governing ballot access, voter registration, vote record-

ing and counting, methods of representation, campaign
funding, and media access. Only then can we break the
two-party monopoly and begin to approximate a genuine
electoral democracy.

★★★

THE POLITICS OF SIN

It's time to talk about sin again. When we were young-sters attending church, the sermons we heard about love and charity were all right, but the ones about sin were really riveting. Sin is a compelling subject, something we can all relate to.

I lived in Washington, D.C., for fourteen years, which might make me something of an expert on sin. Our nation's capital provides a never-ending succession of sinful scandals. Escapades that were once winked at can now ruin public careers. There are scandals about influence-peddling and flesh-peddling, scandals about call girls and call boys. As one comedian commented: "I was shocked to hear that male prostitutes have been asso-ciating with Congressmen, trading sexual favors for money with members of Congress. That's disgusting. It certainly has lowered my opinion of male prostitutes."

Such sin, however, is of the personal kind, the stuff of which tabloid headlines are made, the kind of sin that

Bible-thumping televangelists denounce—when they are not indulging in it. There is another kind of sin that is far worse, but it gets little attention. Yet it hurts more people in serious ways and is more damaging to the social fabric. I am referring to the sins of institutional and class power, whose causes are removed several times from the victim so that the perpetrators are not readily visible. Indeed, the perpetrators do not even see themselves as guilty of any evildoing.

Consider that 15,000 people are killed each year on the job. Millions are disabled, many seriously and permanently, and hundreds of thousands die prematurely from work-related diseases. That is many times more people than are murdered on the streets. Some occupational deaths and injuries are unavoidable but most of them could be prevented by more exacting safety regulations and better enforcement. It is a social evil, a sin, that such conditions prevail.

Consider the children born with birth defects and the adults who are stricken because of exposure to toxic dumps and chemical effluent. A 1980 U.S. Surgeon General's report on toxic chemicals concluded that the air we breathe, the food we eat, and the water we drink together have become the greatest cause of death in America. Yet giant corporations continue to treat our environment like a septic tank, violating pollution and safety standards, giving not a thought to how we might reverse what is swiftly becoming a global catastrophe.

Consider the companies that knowingly market unsafe products, everything from cars to medications to toys; consider the multinational firms that knowingly sell addictive and injurious tobacco products here and abroad — bolstered by U.S. government subsidies — that kill hundreds of thousands every year in the United States alone. Many more people sustain injury, loss, and death from the doings of corporate America than from street crime. There is no social formation more profoundly immoral than a big capitalist corporation. It operates without any scruples and will try to get away with whatever it can.

Vast amounts of money are stolen from the American public by big business through insufficient wages, price-fixing, crooked financing, inflated insurance rates, deceptive sales, and other shadowy practices. Far more money is stolen by these boardroom bandits than by ordinary criminals. The savings-and-loan conspiracy alone cost us more than all the burglaries, bank robberies, and other grand-larceny street crimes in all of America over the past half-century. But unlike crime in the streets, crime in the suites is removed from our immediate perception and is often accomplished by remote control. Though the material and human costs are much worse, the corporate-owned media give far less exposure to corporate crimes than to street crime.

I believe there is such a thing as sin, and it is no mystery what it is. Sin is harmful and hurtful behavior committed by one person against another. Sins can also be committed by organizations, including governments and corporations. Long ago, the Supreme Court created one of its legal fictions by proclaiming corporations to be "persons," entitled to all the rights and privileges of other persons. Nothing in the Constitution supports this strange notion. It is nothing more than a legal fiction to shield directors and chief executive officers from personal responsibility for their crimes—which is why so few of them ever land in jail.

The military is one of the great sinners of our society, although we would never know it, given the esteem and praise heaped upon the armed forces. Military facilities are among the worst environmental violators. Rocky Flats was only one (well-publicized) example of how we are getting poisoned by military nuclear plants. Furthermore, the cost of the war machine makes beggars of us. It seems there is not enough money to help handicapped children and impoverished families, but there is enough for a huge defense budget, the largest single item in the federal budget, allowing the military brass to enjoy a very good life indeed with its officers clubs, golf courses, polo fields, huge salaries, and fat pensions.

The military budget is loaded with bloated contracts, padded cost overruns, and other lavish giveaways to profit-hungry defense firms. The sinners who benefit from all this are the arms profiteers and military brass. The victims are those who perish when bridges and tunnels collapse, the children jammed into overcrowded classrooms, those who go homeless and hungry or who cannot find affordable medical care, and the rest of us who wonder how we can pay all these taxes for missiles, corporate subsidies, and S&L bailouts and still make ends meet. A war machine that is so expensive as to deprive most of us of some modicum of economic security, sapping our ability to improve the life chances of millions of our most vulnerable citizens — such a war machine is a sinful social formation.

What does the military do with all that money? It spends generously upon itself. It wastes billions in corruption and mismanagement. But most of all, it constructs a technology whose goal is to intimidate and subdue people around the world and, if necessary, kill many of them so that their lands and labor can be better put at the disposal of rich owners and foreign investors. The manner of killing has been diluted by the technology — along with the sense of sin. When someone is killed on the street with a gun, it is called murder. But when the killing is performed by long-range missiles or high-altitude jet bombers, the screams are not heard, the mangled bodies are not seen, and sin is not only easily denied but is hailed as a patriotic virtue. Medals are awarded, flags are waved, and greater sums are voted for new weapons systems.

Reality is turned on its head. Aggressive war is called defense. Imperialism is called maintaining our way of life. U.S.-supported death-squad fascism has been used to defend economic privilege in El Salvador, Guatemala, and dozens of other countries, and is called protecting democracy from communism or terrorism.

We need to expand our understanding of sin, and for that matter, virtue, moving from personal piety and interior experience to the realm of social evil and social virtue. This would bring us away from the hypocrisies of the televangelist and closer to the social devotions of the liberation theologist. We need to recognize that members of Congress are at their worst not when cavorting with prostitutes but when they prostitute themselves to moneyed interests that do us real harm.

According to the Bible, not everyone who saith "Lord, Lord" shall enter unto the kingdom of heaven. Personal piety and worshipful proclamations are nice enough, but the really virtuous people in this world are those who work for social justice. They are fighting sin on a grand scale.

BEFORE WE GIVE AWAY
THE POST OFFICE

Free-market conservatives are hostile toward any sector of the economy that performs important social services on a nonprofit basis. Be it libraries, hospitals, schools, colleges, transit systems, or public retirement and disability plans, such services are living demonstration that important human needs can be met collectively in the public sector, without anyone making a profit from them. This is in direct conflict with capitalism itself, which is dedicated to organizing all human activities, all labor and all consumption, in such a way as to maximize the capital accumulation of the owning class. So corporate America and its conservative acolytes in the press and in academia push hard to privatize — and in effect reduce or eliminate — every public service, especially those human services that serve the ordinary public rather than the big corporations.

Consider, for instance, the U.S. Postal Service

(USPS). While people complain about deficiencies in mail service and conservatives urge that the Post Office be privatized, we might ask: What private system would deliver a letter three thousand miles door-to-door within a few days for only the modest price of a first-class stamp? What private business would agree to forward your mail at no extra cost for one year (or longer if you make additional arrangements)?

The Postal Service, which employs over 700,000 people, regularly serves as a scapegoat for incompetence in private business. I can think of occasions when a travel agency, utility company, realtor, publisher, lawyer, and research assistant blamed "the notoriously unreliable Post Office" for delays and disappeared documents — while the fault actually rested with the person uttering the alibi. Far from being unreliable, the USPS has a delivery reliability very close to 100 percent. How many services can make that claim?

Conservative worshipers of the free-market mythology claim that privatization would reduce the price of services. In fact, United Parcel Service (UPS) and Federal Express (FedEx) charge more for overnight delivery than does the Postal Service. True, some private delivery systems have been able to underprice the USPS but only by paying low wages and refusing to serve markets that are not densely populated.

If the USPS is really all that good, why then does it

have such an undeservedly bad reputation? First of all, costs *have* gone up and service *has* declined over the years. In recent decades the government has shown more interest in cutting down postal services than improving them. Twice-a-day deliveries were long ago abolished. Small rural post offices have been snuffed out. And throughout the country thousands of mail collection boxes have been removed while thousands more are relieved of their contents with less frequency than ever. And through all this, mail volume has increased far out of proportion to the population. While volume grew 150 percent in the decades immediately after World War II, not one new major postal facility was built in a large Eastern city.

In addition, there have been hiring freezes and speedups. In major postal centers, letter sorters have carried double workloads, especially during Christmas season when a twelve-hour day, seven-day week has not been uncommon. No wonder that on-the-job instances of physical collapse, heart attack, and even violence have multiplied.

While services have supposedly been put on a strictly business-like basis, the business community continues to enjoy fat postal subsidies, being able to send billions of pieces of advertising each year through the mails at well below cost. No wonder the U.S. Postal Service has had money problems. Like other domestic services it must endure budgetary squeezes so that there will be more funds for missiles, bombers, and the like. Yet it must continue to service the growing advertising needs of thousands of corporations. Aside from all the junk mail, some 80 percent of first-class delivery is also business mail.

With all the supposed streamlining in personnel and services, the Postal Service has become a top-heavy corporation with the number of management slots multiplying many times over the last thirty years, creating thousands of new highly paid positions for corporate executive types whose mission is to squeeze as much out of the postal worker as possible.

The new postal management says it is attempting to cut costs, but as Sarah Ryan pointed out (*Dollars and Sense* Jan./Feb. 1995), "the postal services being turned over to private contractors are those that are the least costly, most efficient, and most revenue producing." Big corporations like Time Inc. and Lockheed are taking over postal operations, but only the "cream," the high-density delivery market rather than rural service. The later will never turn a profit and so will be left in public hands.

As with armaments, telecommunications, utilities, nuclear power, and other "free-market" areas, so with postal service, the socialistic public sector subsidizes the capitalistic private sector. The latter then crows about how much more cost-effective it is. Thus, over the last thirty years the USPS has spent millions on the research and development of such new mail-sorting technologies as the Optical Character Reader and the Remote Bar Code. Developed at public expense, these technologies have been handed over to private-sector operators who reap the benefit of swift, mechanized sorting procedures.

The private operators not only cash in on the Postal Service's R&D, but they are taking over the Post Office's business itself. Some 40 percent of mail volume is pre-sorted by private companies. In addition, these companies pay wage rates that are far below what USPS employees receive and with fewer, if any, benefits. Various states and municipalities that hope to lure their business then offer the private contractors still more blandishments. Thus, reports Ryan, DynCorp has opened shop in Pennsylvania where it received a $650,000 loan from the state, $2.3 million worth of employment services from the city of York, and a $200,000 grant to build a parking lot. DynCorp reciprocated by offering jobs to mail sorters at $6.12 an hour.

Public services are being parceled out to private companies that hire nonunion employees who receive no benefits and lower wages than the former public employees. Hence the trucks that pick up the mail at airports and cart it to small post offices outside major urban areas are now contracted out to nonunion private carriers. Often using their own rigs, these small private contractors take the job at something less than the salary of a postal driver and without benefits.

At present the Postal Service is the best deal going for the general public, not because of its growing privatization but because of its remaining public service sector. Just recently I sent two packages of roughly similar size from California to New Jersey. One went priority mail for $3.00 via the U.S. Postal Service: it arrived in three days. The other cost $4.50 with UPS ground service: it took a week and a half. For all its faults, the public service was the more efficient and less costly.

Some further comparative shopping can be done in regard to other public versus private services. Consider the drive to privatize public education. Those urban areas that recently attempted to hand their schools over to private corporations ended up with worsened services at higher costs. There is no mystery as to why: the private contractor's prime concern was not educating children but squeezing out the largest possible profit from the enterprise. In the free market you don't really get what you pay for.

Proponents of the free market push for privatization not because public services do not work but because they do. If properly funded, the Postal Service, like public transportation, public libraries, public hospitals, public universities, and public pension and disability plans like Social Security, works very well indeed and quite democratically. By "democratically" I mean the services are equitably distributed, paid for from the public purse, with no privileged interest making an undeserved private profit from them.

The "trouble" with the public sector is that it is living demonstration that all sorts of useful human services can be performed and social needs met without use of the free market, without profiteering, private providers who pilfer the public purse.

Upon winning office, the free marketeers defund the public service, actively subvert it, and preside over its deterioration, while subsidizing the private contractors with R&D assistance, and a host of interest-free loans, grants, and other subsidies—all compliments of the U.S. taxpayer. Then, playing on a popular discontent that is of their own making, they turn to us and say, "See, it doesn't work. We need to privatize." What we really need to privatize are the conservative ideologues in public life who try to foist this agenda on us.

AN UNJUST
ECONOMY

THE DISTRIBUTION OF WEALTH

Most pundits who talk about the American economy rarely mention capitalism, except as a panacea for all social ills, rather than a root cause of many of our problems. Consider how wealth is distributed in the United States. There are those who own the wealth of society, the super-rich families and individuals whom we might call "the owning class," and there are those who are dependent on that class for their employment, "the working class" or if you prefer, "the employee class." These include not only blue-collar workers but just about everyone else who is not independently wealthy.

The distinction between owners and employees is blurred somewhat, to be sure. "Owners" include both the wealthy stockholders of giant corporations and the proprietors of a neighborhood grocery store. However, small proprietors control a relatively tiny portion of the wealth and don't qualify as part of the *corporate* owning class.

While glorified as the purveyors of the entrepreneurial spirit, small businesses are just so many squirrels dancing among elephants: they often are stamped out when markets decline or bigger competitors move in. Over six hundred small and medium-sized businesses go bankrupt every week in the United States.

Among the employee class are professionals and middle-level executives who in income, education, and life-style tend to be identified as "middle class" or "upper-middle class." Then there are entertainment and sports figures, lawyers, doctors, and top executives who earn such lavish incomes that they become in part, or eventually in whole, members of the owning class by investing their surplus wealth and living mostly off the profits of their investments.

You are a member of the owning class when your income is very large and comes mostly from the labor of other people—that is, when others work for you, either in a company you own or by creating the wealth that allows your money and realty investments to increase in value. Hard work seldom makes anyone rich. The secret to wealth is to have others work hard for you. This explains why workers who spend their lives toiling in factories or offices retire with little or no wealth to speak of, while the owners of these businesses, who usually do not work in them at all, can amass riches from such enterprises.

Wealth is created by the labor power of workers. As Adam Smith wrote in 1776, "Labor . . . is alone the ultimate and real standard by which the value of all commodities can at all times and places be estimated and compared. It is their real price; money is their nominal price only." What transforms a tree into a profitable commodity such as paper or furniture is the labor that goes into harvesting the timber, cutting the lumber, and manufacturing, shipping, advertising, and selling the commodity (along with the labor that goes into making the tools, trucks, and whatever else is needed in the production process). For their efforts, workers are paid wages that represent only a portion of the wealth created by their labor. The unpaid portion is expropriated by the owners for personal consumption and further investment.

Workers endure an exploitation of their labor as certainly as do slaves and serfs. It is obvious that slaves work for the enrichment of the master and receive only a bare subsistence. Under feudalism, serfs work numerous days for the lord without compensation; again the exploitation is readily apparent. So with sharecroppers who must give a large portion of their crop to the landowner. Under capitalism, however, the portion taken from the worker is not readily visible. All one sees is a day's pay for a day's work. If wages did represent the total value created by labor, there would be no surplus wealth, no profits for the owner, no great fortunes for those who do not labor.

But don't managers and executives make a contribution to production for which they should be compensated? Yes, if they are performing productive and useful labor for the enterprise, and usually they are paid very well indeed. But income from ownership is apart from salary and apart from labor. It is money you are paid *when not working.* The author of a book, for instance, does not make "profits" on his book; he *earns* an income from the labor of writing it, proportionately much less than the sum going to those who own the publishing house and who do none of the writing, editing, printing, and marketing of books. The sum going to the owners is profits; it is *unearned* income. Profits are what you make when not working.

While corporations are often called "producers," the truth is they produce nothing. They are organizational devices for the accumulation of capital, for making money off labor. The real producers are those who apply their brawn, brains, and talents to the creation of goods and services. The primacy of labor was noted years ago by a Republican president. In a message to Congress, Abraham Lincoln stated: "Labor is prior to and independent of capital. Capital is only the fruit of labor and could not have existed had not labor first existed. Labor is the superior of capital and deserves much the higher consideration." Lincoln's words went largely unheeded. The dominance of capital over labor remains the essence of the U.S. corporate system, bringing ever greater concentrations of wealth and power into the hands of a small moneyed class.

Contrary to the prevailing myth, this country's wealth does not belong to a broad middle class. The top 10 percent of American households own 98 percent of the tax-exempt state and local bonds, 94 percent of business assets, 95 percent of the value of all trusts. The richest 1 percent own 60 percent of all corporate stock and fully 60 percent of all business assets, while 90 percent of American families have little or no net assets. The greatest source of individual wealth is inheritance. If you are not rich, it is probably because you lacked the foresight and initiative to pick the right parents at birth.

The push is toward greater economic inequality. In the last fifteen years, income from investments and property (i.e., interest, dividends, rents, land, and mineral royalties) has been growing two to three times faster than income from work. The top 500,000 people have more wealth, more money, than the other 200,000,000. The top 1 percent saw their average incomes soar by over 85 percent after taxes in the last 15 years, while the incomes of the bottom fifth declined by 10 percent. And the trend has accelerated since then. Income and wealth disparities are greater today than at any time in the half-century that such information has been collected. As one economist put it: "If we made an income pyramid out of a child's building blocks, with each layer portraying $1,000 of income, the very richest would be far higher than the Eiffel Tower, but almost all of us would be within a yard off the ground."

Next time you hear politicians and pundits describe America as a middle-class nation, you might wonder what they are talking about. Such concentrated wealth translates into concentrated power over our political, social, and cultural lives and poses a threat to democracy itself.

KEEPING THE RICH
INVISIBLE

When a middle-aged acquaintance of mine bragged that he weighed the same today as he did in his youth, I reminded him that weight resembles wealth: it's not merely the aggregate accumulation that counts, it's the distribution. But wealth differs from weight in that it tends to accumulate at the top. Karl Marx had it right: wealth is becoming increasingly concentrated in the hands of the few, while poverty spreads ever more widely among those below.

Some opinion makers disagree strongly. They insist that ours is a prosperous middle-class society and that our economy is performing well. But, again, look at the distribution. *Cui bono?* Who benefits? During Reagan-Bush-Clinton era, the share of the national income going to those who work for a living shrank by over 12 percent. The share pocketed by those who live principally off their investments increased almost 35 percent. The *New York Times* (June 6, 1996) reported that income disparity in 1995 "was wider than it has been since the end of World War II." Over the last two decades, the average income for the top 20 percent jumped from $73,754 to $105,945 in constant dollars, while the bottom 20 percent moved only from $7,202 to $7,762. But these figures greatly understate the problem.

Put simply, the *Times* story is based on a Census Bureau study that completely excludes the income of the very rich. An average income for the top quintile of $105,945 hardly represents a rich, let alone super-rich, cohort. What goes on here? What has happened to the really rich people?

The remarkable thing is that for years the Census Bureau never interviewed anyone who had an income higher than $300,000; or if interviewed, they were never recorded as above the "reportable upper limit" of $300,000, the top figure allowed by the bureau's computer program. In 1994, the bureau lifted the upper limit to $1 million. This still leaves out the richest 1 percent, the hundreds of billionaires and thousands of multimillionaires who make many times more than $1 million a year—and who own most of the nation's wealth.

By designating the (decapitated) top 20 percent of the entire nation as the "richest," the Census Bureau is including literally millions of professionals and others who make as little as $70,000 or so, people who are anything but the "richest," while excluding the really big money. The super-rich are concentrated in a portion of the population so minuscule as to be judged statistically insignificant. Despite their tiny numbers, they own the lion's share of everything there is to own and enjoy an income advantage thousands of times greater than the spread allowed by the bureau's figures. The difference between a multibillionaire who takes in $100 million in any one year and a janitor who makes $8,000 is not 14 to 1 (the usually reported spread between highest and lowest quintiles) but over 14,000 to 1.

When asked why this sampling procedure was used, a bureau official told my research assistant that the bureau's computers could not handle higher amounts. A most improbable excuse, since once the Census Bureau decided to raise the upper limit from $300,000 to $1 million it did so without any difficulty, and it could do so again.

Another reason the official gave was "confidentiality." Given place coordinates, someone with a very high income might be identified. Furthermore, he said, high-income respondents understate their income. The earnings they report are only about 50 to 60 percent of actual investment returns. In any case, since their actual numbers are so few, they are likely not to show up in a national sample. In a word, studies of this sort give us no idea how rich the very rich really are.

Of late, much media attention has been given to the CEOs who rake in tens of millions of dollars annually in salaries and perks. But little is said about the tens of *billions* these same corporations distribute to their affluent shareholders each year. Publicity that focuses exclusively on a handful of greedy top managers conveniently avoids any exposure of the super-rich. In fact, reining in the CEOs who cut into the shareholders' take would well serve the shareholders' interests.

Marx's prediction about the growing gap between rich and poor still haunts the land — and the entire planet. The number of persons living below the poverty level in the United States climbed from 24 million in 1977 to over 35 million by 1995, with tens of millions more living just barely above the poverty level. And what is called the "poverty level" itself is set at an unrealistically low level that does not take into account the full effect of inflation on basic essentials such as food, fuel, housing, and health, the things that compose a disproportionate amount of the income of low-wage households.

The concentration of wealth creates more poverty. As some few get richer, more people are falling more deeply into poverty than in earlier times and finding it increasingly difficult to emerge from it. The same pattern holds throughout most of the world. For years now, as wealth concentrates globally, the number of poor has been increasing at a faster rate than the earth's population.

Rather than declaring Marx outdated — a pronunci-amento that has been bouncing around the free-market world for over a hundred years — we should note that on some questions he is more relevant than ever. But to understand how so, we have to move beyond the U.S. Census Bureau's cooked statistics.

A FREE MARKET
FOR WHOM?

In the modern capitalist system, wealth is accumulated not only by individual tycoons but by giant multinational corporations. As C. Wright Mills noted, "Not great fortunes, but great corporations are the most important units of wealth, and to these units individuals with big money are variously attached." As Marx predicted over 150 years ago, these units of wealth continue to merge in increasingly greater concentrations. But there is something more to capitalism than just the concentration of wealth. Vast fortunes existed in ancient Egypt, feudal Europe, and other early class societies. What is unique about capitalism is its perpetual dynamic of capital accumulation and expansion—and the dominant role this process plays in the economic order.

Capitalists like to say they are "putting their money to work," but money as such cannot work and cannot create wealth. What capitalists really mean is that they are putting more human labor power to work, paying workers less in wages than they produce in value, thereby siphoning off more profit for themselves. That's how money "grows." The average private-sector employee works a little over two hours for himself or herself and almost six hours for the owners. That latter portion is the "surplus value," that Marx saw as the source of the owner's wealth. Capitalists talk about surplus value all the time. They call it "added value," which is roughly the same thing. Consider the *New York Times* business page advertisement to lure investments to the Big Apple: "New York's manufacturing workers produce $4.25 in value over and above every dollar they get in wages." It might be noted that workers in Texas produce $5 in added value for every wage dollar. And the percentage is substantially higher in most Third World nations.

All of Rockefeller's capital could not build a house or a machine, only human labor can do that. Of itself, capital cannot produce anything; it is the thing that is produced by labor. The ultimate purpose of the free market is to create not "use value" but "exchange value," not useful things but profitable ones. The goal is not to produce goods and services for human needs per se but to make money for the investor. Money harnesses labor in order to convert itself into goods and services that will bring in still more money. Capital annexes living labor in order to create more capital.

The function of the corporation is not to perform public services but to make as large a return on investment as possible. The social uses of the product and its effects upon human well-being and the natural environment win consideration in capitalist production, if at all, only to the extent that they don't violate the profit goals of the corporation. As David Roderick, the president of U.S. Steel (now USX) put it: "United States Steel Corporation is not in the business of making steel. We're in the business of making profits."

This relentless pursuit of profit results from something more than just greed, although there is plenty of that. Under capitalism, enterprises must expand in order to survive. To stand still amid growth is to decline, not only relatively but absolutely. A slow-growth firm is less able to move into new markets, hold onto old ones, command investment capital, and control suppliers. Eventually, slow growth leads to a company's decline. Even the biggest corporations are driven by the need to expand, to find new ways of making money. Ultimately, the only certainty, even for the giants, is uncertainty. Survival can never be taken for granted. **//**

Business leaders correctly point out that they could not survive if they tried to feed or house the poor, or invest in nonprofit projects for the environment or in something so nebulous as a desire to "advance public well-being." Nor can they invest simply to "create more jobs." In fact, many of their labor-saving devices and overseas investments are designed to eliminate jobs and reduce wages.

As unemployment climbs, buying power and sales decline, inventories accumulate, investment opportunities recede, more layoffs are imposed, and recession deepens. For the big capitalists, however, recessions are not unmitigated disasters. Weaker competitors are weeded out and business is better able to resist labor demands, forcing workers to accept wage and benefit cutbacks in order to hang onto their jobs. A large reserve supply of unemployed workers helps to deflate wages. Unions are weakened and often broken, strike activity declines, and profits rise faster than wages. The idea that all Americans are in the same boat, experiencing good and bad times together, should be put to rest. Even as the economy declines, the rich grow richer not by producing a bigger pie but by grabbing a bigger-than-ever slice of the existing pie. Thus, throughout the 1990s corporate profits reached record levels, as companies squeezed more output from each employee while paying relatively less in wages and benefits.

In 1997, inflation was down and employment was up. Yet for the mass of working people real income showed no gains, benefits were cut back, and many worked harder than ever to stay afloat. The bulk of the prosperity went to the few, not to the many. A common problem of modern capitalism is inflation. The 4 or 5 percent inflation rate that has regularly plagued our economy can, in a few years, substantially reduce the buying power of wage earners and people on fixed incomes. Corporate leaders maintain that inflation is caused by the wage demands of labor unions. In fact, wages have not kept pace with prices and profits. Over the past two decades, except for a few brief intervals, inflation has climbed faster than wages, thereby cutting into the buying power and living standard of most workers.

Hardest hit by inflation are the four essentials, which devour 70 percent of the average family income: food, fuel, housing, and health care. But in these and most other industries the portion of production costs devoted to wages over the last decade has been shrinking, while the share taken by executive salaries, stockholders, and interest payments to bankers has multiplied dramatically. The "wage-price" spiral is more often a profit-price spiral, with the worker more the *victim* of inflation than the cause of it.

Those who insist that the free market can answer our needs seem to overlook the fact that the free market has no such interest in doing so. That is not what it is about. The free market's function is to produce the biggest profits possible for its investors. People may need food or housing, but they offer no market until their need is coupled with buying power to become *demand*.

Meanwhile, right-wing ideologues take aim at any human service or entitlement that helps common people. As they see it, everything should go into the free market. Working people do not need public pensions, public hospitals, public libraries, public parks, or public services of any kind. They should place their faith in the free market. The problem is, the free market is not free at all—except for those who compose the investor class. It is not even a market, being dominated by a relatively few rich cartels. It is not there to serve our human or social needs but to maximize profits, making more and more for the few who have so much already and who want it all.

THE MYTH OF NEUTRALITY: TECHNOLOGY AND MONEY

I recently heard a television network official assert categorically that "technology is inherently neither good nor bad; it depends on how you use it." It could be used for helping or harming society, he claimed. He voiced this notion with such authoritative insistence as to leave the impression that he was the first to have thought of it. In fact, many people stress this point, and they are just as mistaken as he.

Only when one speaks hypothetically does technology achieve neutrality: "It could be used for good or it could be used for evil." Such unspecified references to how it *could* be used overlook the reality of how it actually and regularly *is* used. The truth is, technology is "neutral" only when conceived in the abstract, divorced from the social context in which it develops. But since it develops *only* in a social context and since its application is always purposive, then we must ask, *Cui bono?* Who benefits? And is it at someone else's expense?

Technology is used mostly to maximize the powers and profits of the higher circles. New advances in technology are not neutral things; they impact upon us, our communities, and our environment in often hurtful and regressive ways. Consider a recent example of how technology has been utilized to maximize corporate earnings. Monsanto Co. spent $500 million to develop bovine growth hormone (BGH), a "wonder drug" that induces cows to produce abnormally high amounts of milk. The drug is causing serious illnesses and greater health-maintenance costs for dairy herds, and increased feeding needs and animal waste runoffs that further damage the environment. The cows suffer from infection and malnutrition and must be given even more than the usual ration of antibiotics, all of which gets into the milk we consume. The long-term effects of BGH are not known, but it is suspected of having carcinogenic effects.

The increased milk production induced by BGH is costing taxpayers $100 million a year in additional federal surplus purchases, mostly benefiting a few big dairy producers and, of course, Monsanto. So here is technology used for "good" (increased production of a food) having predictably bad results for the cows, the environment, and perhaps millions of adult and child consumers: "neutral" technology in the social context of a profit-driven system of production—that does not give a damn about consumers, animals, or the environment—produces bad results, as many predicted before the drug ever got on the market.

Developed within an existing social order that is dominated by big government in the service of big business, modern technology takes a form that is anything but neutral. Much research and development is devoted to creating weapons of destruction and instruments of surveillance and control. When over 75 percent of all research and development is financed in whole or part by the Pentagon, then it is time to stop talking about technology as a neutral instrumentality and see how it takes form and definition in a context of money and power that gives every advantage to the special interests of the military-industrial complex, the profit-gouging defense industry, and state agencies of control, coercion, and surveillance, all at taxpayers' expense. Meanwhile, the rest of us pony up the funds to pay for it all, while suffering the consequences.

The myth of neutral instrumentality is also applied to money. When I studied economics in school I was taught that money was "a medium of exchange," a neutral mechanism if ever there was one. But such a neutral-sounding definition hides a host of troublesome realities. In fact, money circulates within a particular social context, and like technology, it has a feedback effect of its own, advantaging the already advantaged.

Money creates a way of liquefying and mobilizing wealth. With mobility comes greater opportunities for accumulation and concentration. Before money, wealth could only be accumulated as real property (land) and edifices, livestock, horses, gems, furs, finery, and other luxury artifacts. The advent of precious metals was the first great step to a mobile form of wealth that allowed for greater accumulation and a still greater command over the labor and loyalty of masses of people, themselves bereft of land and capital.

With the growing concentration of wealth and the emergence of a moneyed class there comes a greater concentration and command over technology itself by that class. In a word, big money finances big technology. No wonder that technology, in turn, is developed with an eye to enriching and making the world safe for those who have the money.

What if, instead of defining money in that benign and neutral way, as a medium of exchange, we defined it as "an instrument for the mobility and accumulation of capital and the concentration of economic power"? That would give us a whole new slant on things. Money allows for a level of accumulation and investment previously unknown.

Again, hypothetically speaking, money is just an instrument of exchange that "could" be used for good or bad, for medicine or murder. And to be sure, in everyday life we do use it for necessary and often good things like food and shelter. But looking at the larger picture, money best serves those who have large amounts of it and who use it to accumulate power in order to accumulate still more money.

One could go on with other specific cultural artifacts and institutional arrangements: guns, vehicles, the military, education, and even what is called "culture." Rather than mouthing the truism that these things can be used for good or bad, it is more useful to recognize that such instrumentalities do not exist as abstractions but gather definition only within a social order. Thus the instrumentality not only has all the potential biases and distortions of that order but it contributes distortions and injustices of its own.

It is not very helpful to say that technology or money "could" be used for good or bad. We have to determine why things like technology and money most often are applied to such ill effect. But that would bring us to a radical analysis of the politico-economic system itself, a subject that is avoided like the plague even by most of those investigators who expose the symptomatic abuses of that system.

MURDER ON THE JOB

As everyone knows, the way to amass wealth in a business is to make the largest profit possible. But where do profits come from? Profits are the difference between the value that the workers produce with their labor and the value paid to them and other production costs. The difference between business earnings and labor costs is called "surplus value" by Marxists and "added value" by capitalists. Though the two terms are not used in identical ways, they are close enough to be treated alike.

In the last forty years the rate of surplus value accumulation in U.S. manufacturing increased by almost 300 percent. Thus, in 1954, for every dollar paid in wages, $1.62 was made by the business owners. By 1994, for every dollar paid to the people who do the work, $4.25 was pocketed by those who do not work. A worker who labors for ten hours gets paid for the value produced for less than two of those hours. For some companies the surplus value ratio has been even more lopsided.

Throughout the country, big corporations are downsizing their workforces while maintaining or expanding production levels. The inevitable tendency of profit-driven firms is to extract as much value as possible from labor. The resulting speedup creates greater stress, injury, and illness, for those who do the work. To take a specific instance, General Motors has been cutting hundreds of jobs in various plants "putting immense strain on the workers still there," according to *Economic Notes* (May 1997). The workers are demanding that more people be hired to ease workloads and provide relief. One would think GM had its back to the wall in the highly competitive auto vehicle market. In fact, the company is sitting on a $14.6 billion cash reserve and is raking in juicy profits.

For employees, the picture is less rosy. The April/May 1997 issue of *Solidarity*, a publication of the United Auto Workers Union, features a two-page spread of color photographs of ten UAW auto workers: six white males, one young white woman, and three African American males. What they all had in common was that they were killed on the job in 1996:

James Wacker, 49, St. Louis, Missouri, crushed when demolition material on a lift truck fell on him.

Eddie McCorkle, 37, Melrose Park, Illinois, died of electric shock while tightening connections on a 13,500-volt transformer.

Mike Carlini, 52, Utica, Michigan, crushed between a sprinkler pipe and the guard rail of an elevated scissors lift.

Larry McKinstry, 39, South Bend, Indiana, killed by gunshot while working as a plant security guard.

Ron England, 62, Minneapolis, Minnesota, burned by molten metal flowing out of a cracked, free-standing mold.

Doyle Hurd, 63, Dayton, Ohio, struck by a head cover blown off a forging machine adjacent to his work area.

Lori Ohlinger, 24, Lyons, Ohio, crushed by falling parts from a bin stacked near her work area.

Michael Perry, 46, Tiffin, Ohio, electrocuted in a substation outside the plant.

Neal Weller, 45, Waterloo, Iowa, severely burned from a molten metal eruption while cooling a furnace pour spout.

Leslie King, 41, Conway, Arkansas, crushed by a 3-ton steel coil while checking material in a warehouse.

Statistics are one thing; it is something else to gaze on the pleasantly smiling human faces in the photos. How many pages would it take to print the photos of all the workers who were killed on the job in any one year? Every year in this country over 11,000 meet death at the workplace. There are an additional 1.8 million job injuries annually; 60,000 workers sustain permanent disability; and millions more suffer cumulative disabilities and other work-related illnesses, some 50,000 of whom die prematurely each year from occupationally related diseases. The casualty rate among working people is higher than anything the nation suffered during the Vietnam War — yet we hear hardly a murmur about it in the corporate-owned media.

Industrial work always carries some risk. Some accidents can be blamed on the mistaken judgment of workers. But most of the present carnage is due to inadequate safety standards and lax enforcement of codes, along with the workplace exhaustion, stress, and danger caused by management's speedups and cutbacks. Nor should this surprise us, once we see that the core concern of corporate America is to maximize profit by squeezing as much value out of labor as possible. Every dollar a company spends on safety for workers (and consumers) is one dollar less in profits. From a capital accumulation perspective, it is perfectly rational to skimp on safety.

The same holds true for agricultural work. Agribusiness employers will provide sprinkler systems for crop irrigation but no running water for the shacks their workers are made to inhabit. They will hire veterinarians to attend to their domestic herds but offer no medical care for laborers. The rich growers get crop subsidies and land subsidies, but the impoverished workers do not have adequate unemployment insurance or other benefits. Representing a capital investment, the animals and equipment are treated better than the workers and their families, who are easily replaceable.

Organized labor has fought long and hard for safer work conditions. In 1970, Congress finally created the Occupational Safety and Health Administration (OSHA). Within a matter of years, OSHA effected substantial drops in accidents and sickness. Thus the number of workers killed today is about one-third what it was in 1930, even though the workforce is several times larger. Who says government regulation does not make a difference? If it did not, it would not be so vehemently opposed by big business. In 1996, corporate America tried hard to gut the OSHA law in a series of "reforms" that failed to get through Congress.

If anything, OSHA should be expanded many times over. The agency's resources remain vastly insufficient. At least one in three autoworkers is injured or made ill on the job each year, one in ten seriously enough to lose time from work. But OSHA has only 1,800 inspectors for six million workplaces and 90 million workers nationwide, an average of one inspection per workplace every seventy years.

Worker compensation laws usually place the burden of proof on the injured employee, provide no penalties when industry withholds or destroys evidence, and impose a statute of limitation that makes it difficult to collect on diseases that have a long latency period. Only about 10 percent of the millions of workers injured actually win any benefits. And those who receive compensation forfeit their right to sue a negligent employer. Thus, the government compensation program actually shields industry from liability.

Corporate capitalism is a profoundly immoral system. What does it say about capital enterprise when we need occupational and consumer safeguards? It says that your health and the health of your family means less to the corporate producer than their profits. What does it say about them when inspectors are bribed and safety records falsified? It says that, as with any murderous thief or heartless thug, the value of life is held in lower regard than the pursuit of gain. The companies are without moral scruples worthy of the name. They will try to get away with anything they can, regardless of the cost in human blood and suffering.

The captains of corporate America are regularly impelled by the crassest, most unprincipled, overweening self-interest. They deliberately underreport injuries and fatalities, cooking their records like the unprincipled liars they are. When caught in violations, they often find it less expensive to pay the relatively light fines—frequently renegotiated and greatly reduced—than to sustain the production costs that would bring better safety conditions.

Capitalism is a system without a soul, without

humanity. It tries to reduce every human activity to market profitability. It has no loyalty to democracy, family values, culture, Judeo-Christian ethics, ordinary folks, or any of the other shibboleths mouthed by its public relations representatives on special occasions. It has no loyalty to any nation; its only loyalty is to its own system of capital accumulation. It is not dedicated to "serving the community"; it serves only itself, extracting all it can from the many so that it might give all it can to the few.

Capitalists are always out to make a killing, and they do so in more ways than one.

A GATT TO OUR HEADS

Most Americans know little about the North American Trade Agreement (NAFTA) and even less about the General Agreement on Tariffs and Trade (GATT). And thanks to a virtual media blackout, almost no one has heard of the more recent Multilateral Agreement on Investments. These international agreements all have one thing in common: they are designed to dramatically increase the power of transnational corporations, while undermining consumer and environmental protections, labor unions, democratic sovereignty, and public authority within the many countries that signed the agreements. What we are facing is a silent coup by international monopoly capital, presented to us as a natural, neutral process called "globalization." We are told that nations must undergo this process in order to compete in today's world market.

The true effects of globalization on working people and the environment can be seen in the damage NAFTA already has wreaked upon its three member nations. The Economic Policy Institute estimates that NAFTA eliminated some 600,000 U.S. jobs in its first two-and-a-half years. During that same period, the new jobs created within the United States were mostly in the lower-paying sectors of the U.S. economy. Under NAFTA, wages have fallen in the United States, Mexico, and Canada, and union membership has shrunk dramatically. Canada has lost tens of thousands of well-paying jobs. Companies now can more easily move operations across borders to cheaper labor markets, a threat that has further undermined union organizing and deterred wage demands.

By 1997 NAFTA brought almost a 50-percent increase in the number of maquiladora factories just south of the Mexican border, plants that batten on poverty wages, child labor, and miserable work conditions. Of the 2.5 million Mexican children ages 6 to 14, many do not attend school despite the compulsory attendance rule, and many are child laborers. Since NAFTA, incomes of poor Mexicans have been halved, poverty has spread from 30 to 50 percent of the population, and maquiladora profits have skyrocketed.

NAFTA also brought a precipitous rise in toxic wastes and other environmental devastation. The North American Development Bank, formed ostensibly to decontaminate the maquiladora area, has raised only $2.5 million for a cleanup project that the Sierra Club says will require at least $20 billion. The Commission for Environmental Cooperation (CEC), formed in a NAFTA side agreement supposedly to protect the environment, has refused to take any action against the maquiladoras. Even if the CEC were to rule for a cleanup, it would be the Mexican government's responsibility to carry it out. But the government manifests little determination to act. Like many other Third World countries, Mexico spends hardly a penny on the environment but hundreds of millions of dollars (much of it U.S. aid) in military operations against domestic insurgents.

Then there is GATT. In the Hollywood films of my childhood, a "gat" was a mobster's gun. It is an apt acronym. The Uruguay Round of GATT created an international body, the World Trade Organization (WTO), endowed with sweeping powers to circumvent the sovereignty of all signatory nation states and undermine all governmental laws that attempt to regulate private investment on behalf of the public interest or try to develop not-for-profit public-sector services.

The goal of a transnational corporation is to become truly transnational, poised above the sovereign power of any particular nation, while being serviced by all nations. With GATT, this supranational elevation is practically achieved. Confirmed by no elective body and limited by no conflict-of-interest provisions, the WTO panelists can have financial stakes in the very issues they adjudicate. They are appointed by the heads of various states and are drawn mostly from the corporate world or its adjunct agencies. The WTO's proceedings are shrouded in secrecy; its deliberations and documents are unavailable to public and press. Its rulings are subject to no appeal. The goal is to create a world in which the only regulators are the transnational corporations themselves.

Should a country refuse to change its laws when a WTO panel so dictates, GATT imposes fines and international trade sanctions, depriving the resistant nation of needed markets and materials. GATT benefits strong nations at the expense of weaker ones and rich interests at the expense of the rest of us. It greatly reduces citizen involvement in most important aspects of public policy.

In its first ruling in early 1996, the WTO responded to complaints from Brazil and Venezuela by overturning a section of the U.S. Clean Air Act that prohibited the import of contaminated gasoline (a "nontariff restriction on trade"). Usually the United States is the aggressor in WTO complaints. It sued the European Union for banning the import of meat treated with growth hormones and for giving preference to small Caribbean banana companies over Chiquita, a giant transnational. In both cases, the United States was victorious. The European Union now must accept possibly dangerous, hormone-laden meat and must allow Chiquita full and equal access to its markets, in effect condemning many small banana companies to bankruptcy. The decision in favor of Chiquita is certain to lead to increased unemployment among Caribbean workers, greater illegal immigration to other lands, and—with more desperate economic conditions—an expanded drug trade. (It is speculated that Chiquita chairman Carl Lindner's $500,000 donation to the Democratic Party encouraged Clinton and his trade representative Mickey Kantor to overlook the advice of their drug policy analysts.)

All of GATT's prohibitions are directed against public authority; all its protections are on behalf of private corporate power. The WTO refuses to link trade pacts to workers' rights, including the right to organize. It refuses to abolish or even restrict child labor, lifting not a finger to protect the more than 300 million children around the world, some as young as 5 and 6, who work ten to fifteen hours a day enduring terrible mistreatment under horrendous conditions.

Under the gun of GATT, the ban that Denmark imposed on imported products made in part or whole from endangered species is overthrown as "a restraint of trade." The attempt to have a public single-payer auto insurance system in Canada is ruled unfair competition against private insurance companies elsewhere. And U.S. corporations that provide health insurance to their employees in the United States are moving against the Canadian public health insurance system as "unfair competition." The refusal of the state of Massachusetts and some U.S. cities to contract with companies that do business with a human-rights violator like Burma (selective purchasing laws) are now treated as restrictions on trade. Had this been the rule during the selective-purchasing campaign against South Africa, Nelson Mandela might still be in jail, according to some public-interest advocates.

Increasingly, nations are abandoning their public interest laws at the mere threat of a WTO challenge. Guatemala had some strict laws aimed at protecting the lives of infants by promoting breast-feeding over breast-milk substitutes (the latter lacking the life-saving properties that mother's milk is thought to have). Faced with a WTO challenge, induced by Gerber Products, a producer of baby foods, the Guatemala Supreme Court suddenly ruled that the laws do not apply to imports, a decision that endangers the lives of infants.

The newest subterfuge for undermining our constitution and advancing the cause of international capital is the Multinational Agreement on Investments (MAI), which at the time of this writing (August 1997) is being negotiated among twenty-nine of the world's richest nations. MAI will accord political rights to corporations equal to those of nation-states and prevent nations from limiting foreign investment in any way. Until now, corporations have had to appeal to their governments to challenge irksome laws in other lands. Under MAI, they will be able to sue governments directly before international tribunals that are well stocked with sympathetic adjudicators.

Under the guise of protecting investors' rights, MAI would ban laws that (1) require transnational firms to form partnerships with local companies or employ local managers; (2) subsidize home-grown businesses and limit foreign ownership of local resources; (3) link public subsidies and tax breaks to a corporation's behavior. This last provision would abolish or preempt laws that require subsidized firms to contract union labor, provide a living wage, meet job-creation goals, and reinvest in the local community or in underserved areas.

In sum, these international agreements are undermining public authority and popular sovereignty in the various nations, creating more poverty for the many and more wealth for the few, and more unaccountable corporate profiteering.

Globalization—defined as that process of supranational investor supremacy in all matters of public policy—is neither automatic nor "natural" nor historically inevitable. And it is a process that is far from complete. While investment becomes increasingly internationalized, most manufacturing is still nationally based. The nation-state remains the main conduit through which multinational capital inserts itself into the global market.

As the building block for globalization, the nation-state remains an arena of struggle, a choke point on the lifeline of international capital.

Modern ruling classes prefer to hide their privileges from public view and pretend a devotion to democracy. Our task is not to wage a class war but to realize that class war is being waged against us constantly. More international cooperation between labor unions, progressive organizations, and other popular movements is necessary. The ruling classes have taken the struggle to the international level and we must meet them there to prevent our standard of living, our sovereignty, our rights, and indeed our planet, from being sacrificed to a rapaciously profit-driven, monopoly capitalism.

ECOLOGY FOR THE MONEY

Years ago in New England, a group of environmentalists asked a corporate executive how his company could justify dumping its raw industrial effluent into a nearby river. The river had taken Mother Nature millions of years to build. It had been used for drinking water, fishing, swimming, and other recreational activities. The paper mill had turned it into an open sewer.

The executive shrugged and said that river dumping was the most "cost-efficient" way of removing the mill's wastes. It enabled the company to give the public a quality product at a reasonable price. And it allowed the company to make an "adequate" profit. Furthermore, if the mill had to absorb the additional production costs of disposing of the waste, it just might not be able to maintain its competitive edge and would then have to go out of business, resulting in the loss of jobs.

It was a familiar argument: the company had no choice; it was compelled by the imperatives of a competitive market. Perhaps it never occurred to the executive that if *all* companies were subjected to the same stringent environmental controls and costs, then the additional costs to his firm would not cause it to suffer any loss in its competitive position. But it would still mean less profit for all the polluters.

Profits are the name of the game, as business leaders make clear when pressed on the point. You're not going to stay around very long, they say, if you don't make a profit. The first rule of corporate capitalist production is: make the largest possible profit or eventually go out of business. The central overriding purpose of business is capital accumulation. You must have more capital when you finish than when you began. How could it be otherwise?

This explains why pollution, like sin, is regularly denounced but vigorously practiced. Strip-mining and deforestation by coal and timber companies continue to ruin our forests. It is profitable. Six million acres of topsoil are eroded each year in the United States by chemicalized farming. Industry introduces some one thousand new chemicals into the marketplace annually, often with insufficient or fraudulent information about their effects on health and environment. It is profitable. Billions of pounds of buried toxic wastes, leaking from thousands of sites, contaminate wide areas of groundwater, and cause birth defects, cancer, and other diseases. In all, over one billion pounds of potentially toxic chemicals are released into the environment each day. It cuts costs and is profitable. This situation, say some ecologists, makes the air we breathe, the water we drink, and the food we eat the leading causes of death in the United States. And now the very life-sustaining atmosphere itself is at risk. Chemical compounds deplete the planet's protective ozone layer, making the sun our enemy instead of the source of all life.

There are two critical positions one can take in regard to all this. The first is to say, How irrational and foolish a creature is man that he would foul his own nest. The second, my position, is to acknowledge that ecological devastation is "rational," at least for those who control the land, labor, capital, and technology of society. It is rational in the sense that it is the quickest way to fulfill the central function of business. Environmental devastation continues unabated because production costs are cheaper and profits are higher when industrial wastes can be dumped into the environment and natural resources can be plundered without regard to long-range ecological sustainability.

All the diseconomies of capitalism are foisted on the general populace. The costs of reclaiming the environment, the costs of cleaning up toxic wastes, the costs of monitoring production, the cost of disposing of industrial effluent (which composes 40 to 60 percent of the loads treated by municipal sewer plants), the cost of developing new water sources (while industry and agribusiness consume 80 percent of the nation's daily water supply), and the costs of tending to the sickness and disease caused by pollution do not enter the accounts of industrial firms but are passed on to the public. In this way the private sector can boast of its superior cost efficiency over the public sector.

The overriding function of corporate capital production is not to give you the highest-quality product. Corporations will produce excellent products or cheap, dangerous, useless ones, or both—whatever brings a profit for whatever market. The goal of corporate America is not to produce jobs. Capitalists will create or eliminate jobs, depending on profit considerations. Their intent is not to build communities. They will build or destroy communities, depending on what is to be gained. And certainly, the function of this corporate economy is not to preserve the environment for future generations. For the moneyed interests will treat the environment as a septic tank if it advances the cause of profit making.

To repeat, the core function of capitalism, its raison d'être, is capital accumulation: to accumulate as much money as possible at the highest rate possible. It is not merely a matter of greed, although there is plenty of that. The relentless unyielding hunger for profits is the central operating imperative of the system, the nature of the beast.

Everyone is victimized by environmental contamination, but some more than others. One study found that poor people are more likely to get cancer and other diseases, and more likely to die from them than rich people, partly because the poor have less access to health care and are more likely to delay seeking treatment, but also because the poor take ill at significantly higher rates since they tend to live in areas that are among the most toxic. They are also more likely to work at dirtier, nonunion jobs that offer even less protection from occupational hazards than do unionized worksites.

When I say everyone is affected, I mean the entire world. Industrial effluent is poured into the world's rivers, oceans, and atmosphere by fast-profit, unrestricted multinational corporations operating in Asia, Africa, and Latin America. Third World countries are devastated by mining, timber, and agribusiness companies, adding to the legacy of sickness and poverty in those lands. Poisonous pesticides banned in this country are sold to Third World nations where regulations are weaker or nonexistent. These poisons have an injurious effect on both the workers in the stateside chemical plants where they are made and on agricultural laborers abroad; then they reappear on our dinner tables in the fruit, vegetables, meat, and coffee imported from abroad.

Ecological destruction knows no national boundaries. The search for cheap farmland to raise cattle

1208933

induces agribusiness companies to cut down rain forests throughout Central America. The unusually thin level of topsoil is soon depleted and the land deteriorates from lush forest into scraggly desert. Then the cattle-raisers move on to other forests. The tropical rain forests in Central America and in the Amazon basin are being destroyed at an alarming rate and may be totally obliterated within the next decade. At present, over half the world's forests are gone. Over 25 percent of our prescription drugs are derived from rain forest plants. Rain forests are the winter home for millions of migratory North American songbirds — of which declining numbers are returning from Central America. Many of these birds are essential to pest and rodent control.

The ozone depletion and the dumping of industrial effusions and radioactive wastes into the waterways also may be killing our oceans. If the oceans die, so do we, since they produce most of the earth's oxygen. Today, the carbon dioxide buildup — much of it from automobiles — is transforming the chemical composition of the earth's atmosphere, accelerating the greenhouse effect by melting the earth's polar ice caps and causing potentially cataclysmic climatic aberrations. While the multinational companies are free to roam the world and plunder it almost at will, we are left to suffer the disastrous consequences.

We now know that the earth's capacity to absorb

the heat and poison produced by energy consumption is limited. Ecology is no longer a matter of cleaning up this or that community. The planet itself is at stake. Long before we ever run out of energy sources, we will run out of fresh air, clean water, protective ozone, and climatic stability. We need the following: (1) international controls to protect the oceans and rain forests; (2) development of solar, thermal, tidal, and other alternative energy sources; (3) cutbacks on uses of that ecological disaster, the automobile, and a return to relatively nonpolluting forms of mass transit in and between cities; (4) development of new methods of agricultural production, which in some cases means returning to older, wiser methods.

It could all be done. However, it is not solely a matter of technological choice but of political and economic choices. There is no such thing as "too much" environmental awareness. Only a mass militant ecological movement can hope to save our environment, our Mother Earth, and, yes, our jobs. But it has to be a movement that is willing to confront the environment's powerful profiteering enemies.

A
DANGEROUS
STATE

THE NATIONAL
INSECURITY STATE

Within the government there exists what some have called "the national security state." It consists of the president, the secretaries of State and Defense, the National Security Council, the Joint Chiefs of Staff, and numerous intelligence agencies. The national security state often operates like an unaccountable sovereign power of its own. Its primary function is to defeat political forces that seek alternatives to capitalism at home or abroad or that try to introduce any seriously reformist economic policies, even within the existing capitalist framework.

Making the world safe for free-market capitalism is a massive enterprise. Security agencies expend an estimated $35 billion yearly on operations at home and abroad, if we are to accept the figure bandied about in the press in recent years. Congress has no exact idea how much it allocates for intelligence operations because the total figure is a secret, hidden away under other budget items—in violation of Article I, section 9 of the U.S. Constitution, which reads: "No Money shall be drawn from the Treasury, but in Consequence of Appropriations made by Law; and a regular Statement and Account of the Receipts and Expenditures of all public Money shall be published from time to time."

Of the various agencies of the national security state, the Central Intelligence Agency (CIA) is the most widely known, probably because of its extensive covert actions throughout the world. In addition, there is the Pentagon's Defense Intelligence Agency, which deals with military espionage and counterintelligence; the State Department's Bureau of Intelligence and Research; and the Federal Bureau of Investigation (FBI). Within the Pentagon itself, every echelon—be it the office of the Secretary of Defense, the Army, Navy, or Air Force, or the regional commands around the globe—has its own intelligence service with its own security, communications, and support systems.

While supposedly protecting us from foreign threats, the various intelligence agencies spend a good deal of time policing the U.S. public. They have admitted to maintaining surveillance on members of Congress, the White House, the Treasury and Commerce Departments, and vast numbers of private citizens. They have planted stories in the U.S. media to support their Cold War and counterinsurgency view of the world, secretly enlisting the cooperation of newspaper owners, media network bosses, and hundreds of journalists and editors.

The CIA alone has subsidized the publication of hundreds of books and has owned outright "more than 200 wire services, newspapers, magazines, and book publishing complexes," according to a Senate Intelligence Committee report. The agency has recruited over 5,000 academicians from across the country as spies and researchers, secretly financing and censoring their work. CIA agents participate in academic conferences and the agency conducts its own resident-scholar programs. It offers internships and tuition assistance to undergraduate and graduate students while they are still attending school.

Intelligence agencies have infiltrated and financed student, labor, scientific, and peace groups. The CIA has financed research on mind-control drugs, sometimes on unsuspecting persons, and was responsible for the death of at least one government employee who was driven to suicide after unknowingly being subjected to mind-altering drugs. Erstwhile CIA director Stansfield Turner said that 149 mind-control projects were carried out at over eighty institutions over twenty-five years.

In violation of the National Security Act of 1947, which states that the CIA "shall have no police, sub-poena, law enforcement or internal security functions," the agency has equipped and trained local police forces in the United States. Under President Reagan's Executive Order 12333, the CIA was authorized to conduct domestic surveillance and covert operations against U.S. citizens both in the United States and abroad. The order (still in effect as of 1998) also authorizes intelligence agencies to train and support local police and enter secret contracts with corporations, academic institutions, and other organizations and individuals.

U.S. intelligence agencies have perpetrated terrible crimes against the peoples of other nations. In countries like Guatemala, Greece, Brazil, Chile, Indonesia, Argentina, Zaire, Haiti, and the Philippines, U.S. national security forces have used military intervention, terror, sabotage, bribery, propaganda, and political disruption to bring down populist or democratically elected governments and install regimes that better suited the needs of global investors, including reactionary dictatorships of the worst sort.

Countries that embarked upon popular revolutions, such as Nicaragua, Mozambique, and Angola, found their economies and peoples devastated by the mass-murder assaults of U.S.-supported mercenary armies. The CIA has sabotaged and stolen elections abroad, waged massive disinformation campaigns, and infiltrated and fractured the trade-union movements of other nations. It has funded and trained secret armies, paramilitary forces, torture squads, and death squads, and pursued destabilization and assassination campaigns against labor, peasant, religious, and student organizations in numerous nations. Jesse Leaf, an ex-CIA agent active in Iran, reported that CIA operatives instructed the Shah's secret police on interrogation "based on German torture techniques from World War II" and that the torture project was "all paid for by the USA" (*New York Times*, Jan. 7, 1979).

After World War II, U.S. intelligence agencies arranged for thousands of Nazi war criminals and thousands of their collaborators to "escape" from Allied custody, supplying them with new identities when necessary, putting them on the U.S. payroll, and using them in repressive operations against the Left in Latin America and elsewhere. "Murderers, far from being exempted from such protection, seem to have been among those most likely to obtain it" (*CovertAction Information Bulletin*, Winter 1986). The father of General John Shalikashvili, President Clinton's choice as chair of the Joint Chief of Staff, fought in a unit organized by the Nazi SS, had only praise for the SS, and yet had no trouble settling in Illinois—despite a law that bans all SS members from entry into this country. A network of Eastern European fascists, anti-Semites, racists, and Nazi collaborators found a home in the ethnic outreach program of the Republican party.

U.S. intelligence agencies have used mobsters, drug dealers, and warlords in their war against those who resist the encroachments of global corporatism. Thus the CIA supplied arms and money to the Italian and Corsican mafias to beat and murder members of communist-led dockworkers unions in Italy and France. After these unions were broken by CIA-backed mob terrorism, the gangsters were given a freer hand in transporting tons of heroin each year from Asia to Western Europe and North America.

The CIA buttressed anticommunist warlords in Southeast Asia and Afghanistan, whose opium production increased tenfold soon after the agency moved into these regions. Likewise, CIA involvement in Central America contributed to the U.S. cocaine epidemic of the 1980s. As the Kerry Senate subcommittee discovered, CIA planes transported guns and supplies to right-wing mercenary troops in Nicaragua and procapitalist military leaders in other countries. The planes then were reloaded with narcotics for the return trip to the United States.

CIA operatives participated with mafia associates and business and political leaders to profit from the multibillion-dollar savings-and-loan swindles. Monies gained from such deals, along with drug money laundered through various banks and other financial institutions, were illegally used to finance CIA covert activities.

In 1982, at the urging of the Reagan administration, Congress passed a law that made it a crime to publish any information that might lead to the disclosure of the identities of present or former intelligence agents and informers, even if the information came from already published sources. Under the law, some journalistic exposures of illegal covert activities themselves became illegal.

Taking all these things into account, and other state-sponsored atrocities and crimes too numerous to mention, we would have to conclude that the national security state is itself a major threat to our freedom and national security.

REPRESSING THE LEFT

Under the guise of defending democracy, U.S. security agencies regularly violate our democratic rights. They especially target people who might adhere to democratic tenets but who do not believe in free-market capitalism, treating them as "un-American" and "subversive." Eventually, almost anyone who actively organizes on behalf of progressive causes becomes an object of suspicion and surveillance.

The law often appears ineffective when directed toward social reforms that benefit the many. But when mobilized against political dissenters, the resources of the law appear boundless. Enforcement is pursued with a punitive vigor that itself becomes lawless. Dissenters have been spied on, raided, threatened, maligned, beaten, murdered, or arrested on trumped-up charges, held on exorbitant bail, and subjected to costly, time-consuming trials that paralyze their organizations, exhaust their funds, and destroy their leadership. So people learn that they are not as free as they thought. If they engage in struggles that challenge privileged interests, they risk being targeted for repression.

One mechanism of repression is the grand jury. Supposedly intended to weigh the state's evidence and protect the innocent from unjustifiable prosecution, the grand jury usually ends up doing whatever the prosecution wants. Grand juries have been used to conduct "fishing expeditions." People with unconventional political views have been required to appear without benefit of counsel and without being told the nature of the investigation. They can be forced to answer any question about political ideas and personal associations or face imprisonment for refusing. The upshot is to turn them into involuntary informers regarding any conversation or activity to which they have been privy.

Another control agency is the Internal Revenue Service (IRS). The General Accounting Office, the investigative agency for Congress, found that some twenty-eight civil rights leaders were audited repeatedly for reasons having little to do with tax collection. The Communist Party had its assets seized and was illegally denied tax exemption for years—while the two major procapitalist parties enjoyed uninterrupted tax exemption. The IRS audited the National Council of Churches, a liberal organization, and various antiwar groups in order to uncover the sources of their support. Prodded by the White House and by conservatives in Congress and even by the CIA, or sometimes acting on its own, the IRS has investigated the Black Panther Party, Students for a Democratic Society, gay rights advocates, environmental groups, investigative journalists, liberal politicians, and many other politically oriented individuals, organizations, and publications.

Disagreement with repressive U.S. policies abroad is often treated as disloyalty. In 1990, when a group of activists and church groups linked to the National Council of Churches ran a newspaper advertisement calling for a suspension of U.S. aid to the oppressive (CIA-supported) Salvadoran government, the Justice Department's criminal division demanded that the organization reveal its sources of support and register as a foreign agent— because its advertisement had supposedly lent support to Marxist guerrillas in El Salvador.

The government often decides which ideas we are to be exposed to from abroad. Laws passed during the McCarthy era permit the State Department and the Immigration and Naturalization Service (INS) to exclude anyone who might be affiliated with communist, anarchist, or "terrorist" groups, or who might in any way engage in activities "prejudicial to the public interest" or harmful to "national security." Every year under these sweeping provisions, dozens of prominent authors, artists, performers, journalists, scientists, and labor union leaders from other countries (especially communist ones) have been denied the right to visit and address audiences in the United States.

Under a 1990 change in the law, supposedly no one can be denied a visa because of ideology, but the State Department and the INS still maintain an ideological "lookout list" of some 345,000 individuals. Persons can be removed from the list if they recant and demonstrate five years of active opposition to communism. For instance, Canadians who want to visit the United States but who have been associated with left groups must formally denounce their past political beliefs, file their fingerprints with the FBI and the Royal Canadian Mounted Police, make pro-American vows, provide proof that they are actively engaged in opposing communism, and provide letters of reference from five persons who are themselves then investigated. The process is demeaning and requires a good deal of time and money.

Officials and operatives of repressive right-wing governments and almost any anticommunist émigré departing from a communist country — including persons who just want to pursue more lucrative careers in the United States — have gained easy entry as visitors or permanent residents. Over the years these have included former Nazis from Germany, Nazi collaborators from Eastern Europe, and Vietnamese, Nicaraguan, Cuban, and Afghani right-wingers and erstwhile terrorists.

In contrast, the *victims* of rightist procapitalist regimes, fleeing political repression in El Salvador, Haiti, Chile, and other U.S.-sponsored client states, have been denied entry and deported back to their countries, often to face jail and death. This seeming inconsistency has an underlying logic: rightists are allowed into the country and leftists are not because the Left generally opposes the capitalist class order, while the Right supports it. In fact, that is the major differentiation between Right and Left.

Though the U.S. government signed the Helsinki accords (the international agreement not to restrict freedom of movement), it continues to impose travel restrictions on its own citizens. Critics of U.S. policy have been denied passports because the State Department decided that their activities were "contrary to the interests of the United States." These include such prominent individuals as journalist William Worthy, artist Rockwell Kent, peace advocate Corliss Lamont, and ex-CIA-agent-cum-critic Philip Agee. Thousands of Americans have been prevented from traveling to Cuba and other communist countries. But there are no restrictions on travel to dictatorships that have capitalist economic systems open to U.S. corporate investment on most favorable terms to the investors.

"Loyalty and security" checks have been used by government agencies to deny public employment to people of an anticapitalist persuasion. According to one Supreme Court decision (*Lloyd Corp. v. Tanner*, 1972), private-sector employees have no First Amendment protection from bosses who might fire them or deny them promotion because of their political views. The court ruled that the First Amendment prohibits the government but not private businesses or institutions from suppressing speech. People with affiliations to anticapitalist groups have been hounded out of jobs in labor unions, academia, entertainment, and various other fields by both private employers and government investigators. Such political purges are usually associated with the McCarthy era of the 1950s. In fact, they continue — in a quieter way — to this day.

During the Vietnam War, protestors were attacked by police on campuses and in cities throughout the country. In Orangeburg, South Carolina, police fired into a peaceful campus demonstration, killing three African American students and wounding twenty-seven others. In 1970, Ohio National Guardsmen killed four students and maimed two others who were participating in an antiwar protest at Kent State University. Ten days later, at the all-black Jackson State College in Mississippi, police opened fire into a women's dormitory where protesting students had congregated, killing two and wounding a dozen others.

In these and other such incidents, law enforcers,

whose lives were never in danger, used lethal weapons against protestors, none of whom was armed. "Impartial investigations" by the very authorities responsible for the killings exonerated the uniformed murderers and their administrative chiefs.

This is not the way citizens in a democracy are supposed to be treated by their government. If this is democracy, who needs dictatorship? The fascist threat comes not from the Christian Right or the militias or this or that grouplet of skinheads but from the national security state itself, the police state within the state.

POLITICAL MURDER, USA

We often think that the United States is free of the political murders and terrorism that characterize other countries. Think again. From 1968 to 1971, in a series of unprovoked attacks in more than ten cities, coordinated with the FBI, police raided the headquarters of the Black Panther Party (a Marxist revolutionary organization), wrecking offices, smashing typewriters, stealing thousands of dollars in funds, and arresting, beating, and shooting the occupants. At least thirty-four Panthers were murdered by police in that period, including Chicago leader Fred Hampton, who was shot while asleep in his bed.

Through much of the 1970s, a paramilitary "peacekeeping" force, established by the U.S. Bureau of Indian Affairs under FBI direction, carried out a terrorist campaign on the Pine Ridge Reservation that was directly responsible for hundreds of assaults and the deaths of more than sixty supporters of the American Indian Movement.

The Senate Intelligence Committee revealed that the FBI organized forty-one Ku Klux Klan chapters in North Carolina. FBI informants in the Klan did nothing to stop Klan members and Nazis who committed murder and other acts of violence. In some instances, as in Greensboro, North Carolina, they assisted the murderers by procuring weapons for them and directing them to the correct location.

In Chicago, after repeated death threats, Chicano union organizer and communist Rudy Lozano, who worked effectively to unite Latinos, African Americans, and whites around working-class causes, was shot dead in his home by someone who came to his door on the pretense of asking for a drink of water and who stole nothing. According to family members, paramedics thought they could save Lozano's life, but police blocked them from getting near him, because "evidence might be destroyed."

When two Chicano socialists were killed by bombs planted in their cars, the FBI made no arrests. After a series of threats, an antinuclear organizer was shot dead in Houston and an assistant was seriously wounded; police came up with not a clue.

When agents of the Philippine dictator Ferdinand Marcos conducted operations against Filipino dissidents in the United States, the FBI cooperated with them. One FBI informant admits to having witnessed the murder of two Filipino union leaders who were prominent in the anti-Marcos movement in this country.

The FBI supplied El Salvador's security forces with the names of Salvadoran refugees who were about to be deported from the United States — so that the security police could apprehend them upon their return. Many of these refugees had fled here in the hope of escaping torture and death. Salvadoran activists in this country have endured death threats, assaults, kidnappings, car smashings, and break-ins. The police make no real attempts at apprehending the perpetrators.

People in the Cuban American community who have advocated a more conciliatory policy toward the Cuban government have been subjected to threats and attacks. An anticommunist Cuban exile terrorist group claimed credit for some twenty-one bombings between 1975 and 1980 and for the murder of a Cuban diplomat in New York. Yet the group escaped arrest in all but two instances. A car bombing in Miami that cost a Cuban radio news director both his legs also remains unsolved.

Likewise, three Haitian talk-show hosts in Miami, who aired critical commentaries about military repression in Haiti, were shot dead between 1991 and 1993. The police saw no political motive or pattern to the killings and made no arrests.

In the United States, from 1981 to 1986, there were eleven fatal shootings of Vietnamese publishers, journalists, and activists who had advocated normal relations with the communist government of Vietnam. In each instance, the U.S.-based "Vietnamese Organization to Exterminate Communists and Restore the Nation" (VOECRN) claimed responsibility. One of VOECRN's victims, a publisher of a Vietnamese-language weekly, survived his shooting and identified the gunman, a leader of a Vietnamese extortion gang. The assailant was convicted, but the conviction was reversed at the prosecutor's request because "he had no prior criminal record in this country." Despite VOECRN's communiques claiming responsibility, the FBI saw no pattern or political motive and refused to get involved.

In 1987, after a bombing killed a Vietnamese publisher in California, police finally acknowledged the existence of right-wing Vietnamese terrorism and officially requested FBI assistance. The bureau launched an investigation to determine whether "a pattern is emerging." Imagine, if a dozen corporate business leaders were killed and some radical anticapitalist or anarchist group claimed credit, would the FBI and police wait years and deny that the crimes formed a pattern and were politically motivated? They would have arrested every leftist in sight.

There is the disturbing case of Professor Edward Cooperman, an American, who was shot dead while working in his office at California State University,

Fullerton. As founder of an organization advocating scientific cooperation with Vietnam, Cooperman had received death threats. Lam Van Minh, a Vietnamese émigré and Cooperman's former student, admitted witnessing the professor's death and was arrested. As he tells it, Cooperman produced a gun which accidentally discharged and killed him. Minh left in a panic, for some reason taking the gun with him. He then took a female friend to a movie, after which, he returned to the office and placed the gun in Cooperman's hand. The office had the appearance of a struggle which, Minh's attorney argued, resulted merely from the professor's attempts to get up after being left for dead. The prosecution introduced little to dispute Minh's improbable story. He was convicted only of involuntary manslaughter, sentenced to three years and served one. Minh had been previously arrested for possession of stolen property, at which time police had found guns and ammunition in his car and home. Minh's attorney and legal fees were paid by a Vietnamese linked to right-wing groups.

Other political murders or suspicious deaths in the United States include Alan Berg, a popular Denver talk-show host who engaged in impassioned arguments with anti-Semitic and racist callers and who was shot by members of a white supremacist group; Don Bolles who, at the time of his murder, was investigating a financial scandal said to implicate some of Arizona's most powerful political and business leaders; Karen Silkwood, who was investigating radiation safety negligence at the Kerr-McGee Corporation; and Danny Casolaro, whose investigation of government and business corruption might have implicated high-ranking U.S. officials. None of these murders have been solved or thoroughly investigated.

Then there were the killings of Chicano militants known as the Brown Berets, the murders of Malcom X, Martin Luther King, John Kennedy, and Robert Kennedy, none of which has ever been satisfactorily explained or fully investigated.

The FBI, however, was quick to make arrests when environmentalist Judi Bari was seriously injured by a bomb planted under her car seat in 1990. They arrested the victims, Bari and the other person in the car, Daryl Cherney, calling them "radical activists" and claiming it was their bomb. In fact, both Bari and Cherney were outspoken advocates of nonviolence. The charges were eventually dropped for lack of evidence. The FBI named no other suspects. Bari lived the rest of her days partially disabled and in chronic pain. Never fully recovering her health, she succumbed to cancer in 1997.

Neo-Nazis and skinheads have committed acts of assault, arson, vandalism, and murder throughout the nation. That rightist terrorists repeatedly have been able to perpetrate such crimes and even publicly claim responsibility — without getting caught — means law enforcers have made little effort to monitor and deter their actions, unlike the way they monitor legal and peaceful groups on the Left.

It is worth pointing out that there is nothing inconsistent about this position. Left groups — no matter how nonviolent and lawful — challenge the capitalist system or some aspect of its privileges and abuses, while most right groups — no matter how violent and unlawful — do the dirty work for that system. If they attack federal facilities or banks, the right-wingers might get into trouble. But when they target progressive groups or individuals, they literally can get away with murder. In fact, they are sometimes assisted by federal, state, or local police in their acts of murder.

Again, if this is democracy, who needs fascism?

SAYING "NO" TO LEGALIZED DRUGS

Some people are talking about legalizing the sale of narcotics. This would supposedly take the criminals out of the supply system, the profits out of drug pushing, and the romance out of drug consumption. Certainly, for the pitiful addict who needs both an immediate fix and a gradual rehabilitation, drug consumption should be decriminalized under a controlled-distribution system. But across-the-board legalization is something else. It fails to get at the real problem, which is not the *unlawful* consumption of narcotics but consumption as such. Whether distribution is legal or illegal, the problem is the continual spread of crack, heroin, and other life-damaging narcotics.

It is argued that legalization would take the profits out of drug sales. But when did legalization take the profits out of anything? Tobacco and alcohol, to mention two legalized narcotics, are a source of multibillion-dollar profits. The methadone program, a legalized alternative to heroin, brings in handsome profits for methadone producers, while turning heroin addicts into methadone addicts.

In any case, the major problem is not the profits made by suppliers but the damage done to drug abusers and others in our communities. When something is made legal, it becomes more accessible, and when more accessible, it is consumed more. All we would accomplish by legalizing drugs is to change the suppliers and increase the number of potential consumers. In fact, legalization sometimes does not even eliminate the old suppliers; it does not always take the criminals out of distribution. New York State's legalized lottery has not done away with the numbers racket or other forms of illegal gambling. The availability of methadone has not eliminated heroin. A controlled drug-distribution system would not eliminate opportunities for unlawful distribution — especially to those who remain outside the programs for whatever reasons.

Another feeble argument paraded by legalization advocates is the forbidden-fruit theory, which postulates that the illicit product will lose its attraction once it is legalized. Supposedly multitudes drank during Prohibition simply because liquor was made more exciting by being taboo. Not true; there was a dramatic *decrease* in alcohol consumption during Prohibition. Even with all the bathtub gin and bootleg whisky, per capita alcohol consumption went from about 2.50 gallons in the 1906–1915 era (before World War I) to 0.90 in 1920–1930 (during Prohibition). After Prohibition was repealed in 1934, alcohol consumption swiftly climbed in one year to 1.20 gallons per person, and by 1942–46 it had reached 2.06 (Lender and Martin, *Drinking in America: A History*, pp. 196–7).

Moreover, mortality from cirrhosis of the liver and other alcohol-related diseases was less during the Prohibition era (7.6 to 7.2 deaths per 100,000) than before (13 to 13.5 in 1912–13) and after (8.3 in 1936 and 11.3 in 1960), according to government studies (Census Bureau, *Mortality Statistics*, 1914, 1929, 1934, and *Statistical Abstract of the United States*, 1985).

This demonstrates that commodity availability is a crucial factor in determining consumption, although not the only one. Just look around you: when the liquor stores are closed, liquor sales and consumption go down. There is less drinking in dry counties than in wet ones. With legalization, availability goes up and so does consumption. Our two most dangerous and thoroughly legalized narcotics are alcohol and tobacco. Available just about everywhere, they respectively kill thirty and sixty times more people than does drug abuse. What does this say for legalization? While it would be difficult to successfully outlaw drinking and smoking, measures are being taken to limit advertising and marketing, and restrict the times and places in which alcohol and tobacco can be consumed. In other words, by making them less, not more, available.

The same holds true for gambling: the more available it is, the more people gamble. Legalization did not take the profits out of gambling. It just created new revenues for state governments. Legalization also created new gamblers. In twenty-eight states and the District of Columbia, Americans who would never go to the track or enter an offtrack betting parlor now buy lottery tickets at their grocery stores. This ready availability is reinforced by the splashy, glamorized advertisements and the low price of tickets. It is the easy access to gambling that increases its danger. An economist at Duke University who did a study of state lotteries, maintains that gambling increases the longer the lottery exists in a state. Chronic and compulsive gambling is growing. Legal games stimulate participation not only in state-sponsored gambling but also in illegal gambling. Worse still, it was found that many of these new gamblers are people at the lower economic rungs: poor women, members of minority groups, new immigrants, and teenagers. What does that say for legalization?

People get into drugs not because drugs are illegal and naughty, but because they are accessible and plentiful. Availability remains a necessary condition for all consumption. There is no need to make narcotics still more available for those who are alienated, desperate, impoverished, and demoralized, or who are just bored, curious or thrill-seeking, or immature and coerced by peer pressure.

In regard to drugs and most other commodities, it is always assumed, in keeping with our free-market ideology, that demand creates supply. In fact, things can work the other way around: supply often creates demand. When the British introduced great quantities of opium into China, it was not in response to some popular demand on the part of the Chinese. For the British imperialists, it was a devilishly convenient way of creating a new market and turning a good profit on something produced in one colony (India), while creating passivity and submission among the population of another colony (China). The Opium Wars were an attempt by the Chinese to resist the British importation of a substance that was turning large numbers of Chinese into dope heads. Somehow the Chinese knew that to "just say no" was not enough. So they attacked the British pushers, the big suppliers who were bringing in the stuff and creating a demand.

More recently, during the late 1960s into the 1970s, Israeli military officers were running drug shipments to Egypt, specifically targeting the Egyptian army. As one colonel said, "It allowed us to control and practically avoid drug smuggling into Israel, and increase the use of drugs within the Egyptian army." Egyptian military officials admitted that during that period, drug consumption in the ranks rose by 50 percent (*CovertAction Quarterly*, Spring 1997).

What is to be done regarding our own drug problem? To be sure, we need public education campaigns and rehabilitation centers and massive job and housing programs and other social services for those sectors of the population that are potentially most vulnerable to narcotics infestation. *But we also need to smash the international drug traffic itself.* We need to attack the suppliers, with the severest sanctions reserved for the most important drug merchants. The prime targets should be not the neighborhood pushers but the major suppliers. This is said to be a near impossible task. But a wholesale international war on major traffickers has never really been tried—except in China, Cuba, Indochina, Afghanistan (temporarily), and a few other places where revolutionary communist forces took state power. A war on drugs would not be all that impossible if we really made it our policy and enlisted the efforts of other nations like Pakistan and Thailand, Colombia and Bolivia, getting them to be as tough on the drug traffickers as they are on their own peasants, students, and workers who struggle for social betterment.

Today the CIA plays the same role in this country

and elsewhere as the British did in China. The CIA knows where the harvesting is done in Latin America and Asia. It knows the routes used by major suppliers like the Afghan mujahideen. For years the CIA knew about and actively participated in the large cocaine-smuggling operation between Argentina and the United States and the locations of drug-processing factories in Sicily run by the Inzerillo and Spatola families and their connection to the Gambino family in New York. The CIA even knows which freighters shipped the heroin from Sicily to which ports in the Dominican Republic, and which airstrips in Central America are used for cocaine and where they land in the United States, and which banks at home and abroad launder the billions of dollars. The CIA knows the names of top officials and senior military officers in Ecuador, Venezuela, Colombia, Costa Rica, Guatemala, El Salvador, and elsewhere who pocket large sums to look the other way or who are directly involved in the cocaine trade. The CIA not only has known about such doings, its operatives have participated in the illicit traffic, if we are to believe the evidence brought to light by three different Congressional committees over the last twenty years.

For years cocaine was an expensive professional-class "recreational drug." In the 1980s it began appearing at bargain prices on the inner-city streets in concentrated form as "crack," leading to the coke epidemic that is still with us. Supply created demand, compliments of the CIA.

You do not have to be a conspiracy theorist to wonder what kind of game right-wing policymakers are playing with the drug traffic. In this context I am intrigued by those conservative news columnists, like William Buckley, Jr., who have dismissed the effort against drugs, contradictorily claiming that the drug problem is both highly exaggerated and vastly uncontrollable. These same conservative commentators rail against the corrosion of American values and the destruction of the fabric of our society, yet they seem oddly languid about narcotics.

Nor do I blame them. If I were a right-winger I would have other things to worry about, for instance, the explosive potential of the black and Latino urban proletariat. I would be grateful that the urban uprisings of the sixties have not been repeated, despite the cruel cuts in human services. I would be delighted that the young men on the streets are not talking revolution, as did their counterparts of an earlier generation who joined the Young Lords, Brown Berets, and Black Panthers. And I might not feel upset that it is because they are too busy shooting up themselves with needles and each other with guns.

Not only the youth but entire inner-city communities are under siege, unable to fight effectively for bread-and-butter issues because they have all to do to keep from being submerged in the narcotics tide. Often the police are in the pay of drug lords and are therefore more likely to act against citizens who oppose drugs than against those who push drugs.

Most African American, Latino, and other community leaders have little patience with talk about legalization of drugs. The trouble is that drugs, in effect, already are legalized in that they are readily available in many communities. People want an end to the flood of narcotics coming into their neighborhoods and they want the government to do something about it at the international, national, and local levels.

But it appears the government has another agenda. Drugs are an important instrument of repression and social control. The British imperialists knew this and so do our conservative pundits, the CIA, and the White House.

IS CONSPIRACY ONLY
A THEORY?

Many people suffer from what I would call "conspiracy phobia." They treat anyone who investigates actual conspiracies as an oddball, a "conspiracy buff." They presume without benefit of argument or evidence that conspiracy investigators are dealing with fantasy or kooky imaginings and that what they are saying is patently false. As an article of faith, the conspiracy phobics believe that conspiracies do not exist, or if they do exist, they are of no great significance.

The conspiracy phobics have a nonfalsifiable way of dealing with the question of conspiracy. If someone refers to a clandestine, illegal event, a secret plot or assassination, this is "a conspiracy theory." If the event proves true, such as Watergate or Iran-contra, then, according to the conspiracy phobics, it is not a conspiracy, it is an actuality. In other words, conspiracy can never be proven, for once proven, it is no longer a conspiracy. By definition, conspiracies are imaginary things that never happen.

Now this is a curious thing, especially in view of the fact that conspiracies do exist and are a matter of public record. Conspiracy is even a legitimate concept in law: the collusion of two or more people pursuing illegal means to effect some illegal end. Juries find people guilty of conspiracies. And people go to jail for conspiracies.

The Watergate break-in was a conspiracy, as was the Watergate coverup which led to Nixon's downfall. Iran-contra was a conspiracy. The Joint Congressional Select Committee investigating Iran-contra declared that it was an immense conspiracy and that we would probably never get to the bottom of it. Certainly not the way that committee was investigating it. The savings-and-loan scandal was described by the Justice Department as "a thousand conspiracies of fraud, theft, and bribery." Yet there are people around who say that conspiracies do not exist, who facilely dismiss any critical argument or analysis by labeling it a "conspiracy theory."

The problem is fueled by the fact that there indeed are wacko conspiracies. There are people who believe that the United States is currently being invaded and taken over by a secret UN army transported by black helicopters, or that African Americans, Jews, feminists, gays, cultural elites, and the enemies of family values are taking over the country. But just because there are kooks who believe in imaginary conspiracies does not mean that all conspiracies are imaginary or kooky. Just because there are wackos who ascribe immense power to relatively powerless groups does not mean there are no immensely powerful and even secretive groups.

Often the term "conspiracy" is applied in a dismissive way whenever one tries to ascribe any kind of human agency to elite power. If you suggest that people who occupy positions of enormous economic and political power are willfully dedicated to protecting and advancing their elitist interests, someone will derisively ask, "Oh, what do you have, a conspiracy theory?"

Even when these elites openly profess their designs, there are those who deny that conscious intent is involved. Not long ago I mentioned to an acquaintance that, according to mainstream press reports, the top officers of the Federal Reserve held a national meeting and openly said that they would safeguard against inflation and the overexpansion of the economy by pursuing monetary policies designed to maintain the existing level of unemployment. Like any creditor class, they wanted to keep the economy tight and under control. When I mentioned this to my friend, he said in that patronizing tone that is the mark of superior discernment, "Do you really think they deliberately pursue such a goal? Do you really think they *want* people to be unemployed?" I said, "No, I don't *think* that; they *said* it as quoted in the press." Yet he assumed I was imagining a conspiracy because I ascribed willful and conscious intent to Federal Reserve bankers who admitted to that very same conscious intent, bankers who have such a strong grip on the monetary life of this country.

On another occasion at a World Affairs Council meeting in San Francisco, I said to another participant that a major goal of U.S. policymakers was to implant free-market economies in the former USSR and Eastern Europe. To which he responded skeptically, "Do you really think they carry it to that conscious level?" Again, I had to remind him that I was not ascribing a conspiratorial intent but was reiterating what they themselves had publicly and repeatedly said about the necessity of free-market "reforms" in the former communist nations.

Those who suffer from conspiracy phobia are fond of saying: "Do you actually think there's a group of men sitting around in a room plotting things?" For some strange reason this image of a group of men (usually with no women present) *actually sitting around in a room* is considered so utterly unbelievable. I respond ironically by saying, "No, they meet on carousels or they jump out of airplanes and talk while freefalling." Of course they sit around in rooms. Where else would they meet? They are constantly conferring and they have plenty of rooms at the CIA, the White House, the State Department, the FBI, the Pentagon, the NSA, and wherever else. And yes, they consciously plot to make certain things happen, to overthrow governments, to set up systems of violent repression against reformist or revolutionary governments and movements, to ship arms to clandestine armies. They don't call it plotting, they call it "planning." They have a whole different vocabulary to designate their state-sponsored conspiracies: "secret operations," "covert actions," "deep operations," "off-the-shelf operations," "blackbook operations."

At the broader policy level, no one confabulates and plans more than the political and corporate elites of America. No one does more consciously self-interested policy studies — most of it in secrecy — than they. They have whole professions dedicated to special planning. They spend billions of dollars each year of our tax money to make the world safe for their interests. Yet we have our conspiracy phobics asking us, with incredulous and patronizing smiles, if we really think that the people at the top actually *talk* to each other about their mutual interests and agendas, and intentionally act in pursuit of their interests.

There are those who do not believe that ruling-class conspiracies exist, or even that ruling-class consciousness exists, or even that people at the top have agendas of any kind. What then would they have us believe? That the butcher, the baker, and the barber might consciously pursue their interests but not the banker? That the politician, the policymaker, and the plutocrat have no direction in life? That they never attempt to mislead the public as to what their goals might be because they have no conscious goals? That it is all left to chance and accident? Whence comes this touching faith in random and even somnambulist tendencies of the powers that be?

There are those who do not believe that national security agencies are capable of illegal and sinister acts. What then would they have us believe? That intelligence agencies have nothing to hide from the public and practice secrecy solely to safeguard us from foreign enemies? That they never lie about their intentions and actions, about their complicity with ex-Nazis, and their training of torturers in Indochina and Latin America, their secret arms shipments and their drug trafficking on four different continents?

In 1990 or so, I came across the list of participants in the Bildenberg Conference, an international gathering of those who own and control much of the world. The first two names listed as part of the delegation from the United States were David Rockefeller, of Rockefeller Bros., and the Hon. Bill Clinton, governor of Arkansas. Of course, Rockefeller was no surprise, but I wondered what the governor of Arkansas was doing hobnobbing with international financiers, militarists, and globalization specialists at Bildenberg. A year later, Clinton announced his candidacy for president of the United

States and was immediately hailed by the corporate media as a leading contender for the Democratic nomination, along with another conservative Democrat, Paul Tsongas, former senator from Massachusetts. Then I had a better sense of how Clinton fit into things.

These elites get to know each other. They plant words of ambition and promise in each other's ears. They solicit support, offer reassurances, reach understandings. They meet, talk, and plan—yes, in rooms. Their meetings are usually kept private, as are their agendas. They conspire regularly and frequently. The word "conspiracy" should not be used to dismiss the actuality.

I once saw a cartoon poster of two steers in a meadow. One of them has this anguished expression on its face and is saying, "Oh, I just discovered how they make hamburgers." And the other steer looks at the first with a patronizing smirk and says, "There you go, you leftist paranoids with your conspiracy theories."

MANAGED MEDIA

METHODS OF MEDIA MANIPULATION

According to people in the media industry, some news bias is unavoidable. Distortions are caused by deadline pressures, human misjudgment, budgetary restraints, and the difficulty of reducing a complex story to a concise report. Furthermore, they say, no communication system can hope to report everything; selectivity is needed.

Such problems certainly do exist. But I would argue that the media's misrepresentations are not all the result of innocent error and everyday production snafus. True, the press has to be selective, but what principle of selectivity is involved?

Media bias usually does not occur in random fashion; rather, it moves in the same overall direction again and again, favoring management over labor, corporations over corporate critics, affluent whites over inner-city poor, officialdom over protestors, the two-party monopoly over leftist third parties, privatization and free-market "reforms" over public-sector development, U.S. dominance of the Third World over revolutionary or populist social change, investor globalization over nation-state democracy, national security policy over critics of that policy, and conservative commentators and columnists like Rush Limbaugh and George Will over progressive or populist ones like Jim Hightower and Ralph Nader (not to mention more radical ones).

The built-in biases of the corporate mainstream media faithfully reflect the dominant ideology, seldom straying into territory that might cause discomfort to those who hold political and economic power, including those who own the media or advertise in it. What follows are some common methods of manipulation:

Suppression by omission. Manipulation often lurks in the things left unmentioned. The most common form of media misrepresentation is suppression by omission. Sometimes the omission includes not just vital details of a story but the entire story itself, even ones of major import. Thus the Tylenol poisoning of several people by a deranged individual was treated as big news but the far more sensational story of the industrial brown-lung poisoning of thousands of factory workers by large manufacturing interests (who themselves own or advertise in the major media) has remained suppressed for decades, despite the best efforts of worker safety groups to bring the issue before the public.

We hear plenty about the political repression perpetrated by left-wing governments such as Cuba, but almost nothing about the far more brutal oppression and mass killings perpetrated by U.S.-supported right-wing client states such as Turkey, Indonesia, Saudi Arabia, Morocco, El Salvador, and Guatemala.

The media can mute or downplay truly sensational (as opposed to sensationalistic) stories. Thus, in 1965 the Indonesian military—advised, equipped, trained, and financed by the U.S. military and the CIA—overthrew President Achmed Sukarno and eradicated the Indonesian Communist Party and its allies, killing half a million people (some estimates are as high as a million) in what was the greatest act of political mass murder since the Nazi Holocaust. The generals also destroyed hundreds of clinics, libraries, schools, and community centers that had been opened by the communists. But it took three months before this sensational story received a brief mention in *Time* magazine and yet another month before it was reported in the *New York Times* (April 5, 1966), accompanied by an editorial that praised the Indonesian military for "rightly playing its part with utmost caution."

Information about whole areas of policy, about death squads, massive repression, brutal murder and suppression and torture practiced by U.S.-sponsored surrogate forces in the Third World, and drug trafficking—all

crimes committed by the U.S. national security state—
are for the most part suppressed. They are excluded from
the mainstream media with an efficiency and consistency
that would be called "totalitarian" were it to occur in
some other countries.

Attack and destroy the target. Sometimes a story
won't go away. When omission proves insufficient, the
media move from ignoring the story to vigorously attack-
ing it. So come the hit pieces in the print and broadcast
media, a barrage, unrelenting, repetitive, unforgiving,
backed by a cascade of outright lies.

Over the course of forty years, the CIA involved
itself with drug traffickers in Italy, France, Corsica,
Indochina, Afghanistan, and Central and South America.
Much of this activity was the object of extended con-
gressional investigations—by Senator Frank Church's
Foreign Relations Committee and Congressman Otis
Pike's Select Intelligence Committee in the 1970s, and
Senator John Kerry's Select Committee on Intelligence
in the late 1980s—and is a matter of public record. But
the media seem not to have heard about it.

In August 1996, when the *San Jose Mercury News*
published an in-depth series about the CIA-contra crack
shipments that were flooding East Los Angeles, the
major media held true to form and suppressed the story.
But after the series was circulated around the world on
the Web, the story became too difficult to ignore, and the

media began its assault. Articles in the *Washington Post* and *New York Times* and reports on network television and PBS announced that there was "no evidence" of CIA involvement, that the *Mercury News* series was "bad journalism," and that the public's interest in this subject was the real problem, a matter of gullibility, hysteria, and conspiracy mania. In fact, the *Mercury News* series, drawing from a year-long investigation, cited specific agents and dealers. When placed on the Web, the series was copiously supplemented with pertinent documents and depositions that supported the charge. In response, the mainstream media simply lied, telling the public that such evidence did not exist. By a process of relentless repetition, the major media exonerated the CIA from any involvement in drugs.

Labeling. Like all propagandists, media people seek to prefigure our perception of a subject with positive or negative labeling. Some positive ones are: "stability," "the president's firm leadership," "a strong defense," and "a healthy economy." Indeed, who would want instability, weak presidential leadership, a vulnerable defense, and a sick economy? The label defines the subject, and does so without having to deal with actual particulars that might lead us to a different conclusion.

Some common negative labels are: "leftist guerrillas," "leftist hardliners," "Islamic terrorists," "conspiracy theories," "inner-city gangs," and "civil disturbances."

These, too, are seldom treated within a larger context of social relations and issues. The press itself is facilely and falsely labeled "the liberal media" by the hundreds of conservative columnists, commentators, and talk-show hosts who crowd the communication universe to complain about being shut out of it.

Face-value transmission. One way to lie is to accept at face value what are known to be official lies, uncritically passing them on to the public without adequate confirmation. For the better part of four years, in the early 1950s, the press performed this function for Senator Joseph McCarthy, who went largely unchallenged as he brought charge after charge of "treason" and "communist subversion" against people whom he could not have victimized without the complicity of the national media. Face-value transmission has characterized the press's performance in almost every area of domestic and foreign policy, so much so that journalists have been referred to as "stenographers of power." (Perhaps some labels are well deserved.) When challenged on this, reporters respond that they cannot inject their own personal ideology into their reports. Actually, no one is asking them to. My criticism is that they already do. Their conventional ideological perceptions usually coincide with those of their bosses and with officialdom in general, making them faithful purveyors of the prevailing orthodoxy. This confluence of bias is perceived as "objectivity."

False balancing. In accordance with the canons of good journalism, the press is supposed to tap competing sources to get both sides of an issue. In fact, both sides are seldom accorded equal prominence. One study found that on NPR, supposedly the most liberal of the mainstream media, right-wing spokespeople are often interviewed alone, while liberals — on the less frequent occasions they appear — are almost always offset by conservatives. Furthermore, both sides of a story are not necessarily *all* sides. During the 1980s, television panel discussions on defense policy pitted "experts" who wanted to maintain the existing high levels of military spending against other "experts" who wanted to increase the military budget even more. Seldom if ever heard were those who advocated drastic reductions in the defense budget. Progressive and radical views are virtually shut out.

Framing. The most effective propaganda is that which relies on framing rather than on falsehood. By bending the truth rather than breaking it, using emphasis and other auxiliary embellishments, communicators can create the desired impression without resorting to explicit advocacy and without departing too far from the appearance of objectivity. Framing is achieved in the way the news is packaged, the amount of exposure, the placement (front page or buried within, lead story or last), the tone of presentation (sympathetic or slighting), the headlines and photographs, and, in the case of broadcast media, the accompanying visual and auditory effects.

Newscasters use themselves as auxiliary embellishments. They cultivate a smooth delivery and try to convey an impression of detachment that places them above the rough and tumble of their subject matter. Television commentators and newspaper editorialists and columnists affect a knowing style and tone designed to foster credibility and an aura of certitude, or what might be called authoritative ignorance, as expressed in remarks like "How will this situation end? Only time will tell." Or, "No one can say for sure." (Better translated as, "I don't know and if *I* don't know then nobody does.") Sometimes the aura of authoritative credibility is preserved by palming off trite truisms as penetrating truths. So newscasters learn to fashion sentences like "The space launch will take place as scheduled if no unexpected problems arise" or "Because of lagging voter interest, election-day turnout is expected to be light" or "Unless Congress acts soon, this bill is not likely to go anywhere."

We are not likely to go anywhere as a people and a democracy unless we alert ourselves to the methods of media manipulation that are ingrained in the daily production of news and commentary. The news media regularly fail to provide a range of information and commentary that might help citizens in a democracy develop their own critical perceptions.

The job of the corporate media is to make the communication universe safe for corporate America, telling us what to think about the world before we have a chance to think about it for ourselves. When we understand that news selectivity is likely to favor those who have power, position, and wealth, we move from a liberal complaint about the press's sloppy performance to a radical analysis of how the media serve the ruling circles all too well with much skill and craft.

PACK PUNDITRY

It was back on January 20, 1990, a cold drizzly Saturday afternoon when I was living in Washington, D.C. Sitting in my apartment, I decided to take full advantage of the freedom of choice we Americans are said to enjoy. Which public affairs programs on television should I watch? I checked the "Public Affairs" TV listing and the choice *was* overwhelming in its own way. There was a PBS program called "American Interests" and its guest was Henry Kissinger. It had been quite some time since I had last seen Henry Kissinger holding forth on television — maybe a good forty-eight hours. Kissinger was slated to talk about "Great Power Politics in the 1990s." The 1990s were only twenty days old, so I figured he couldn't have all that much to say. I decided to take a rain check, secure in the knowledge that I could catch Henry whenever I wanted.

The next offering was "Evans and Novak" on CNN. Those two conservative syndicated columnists were interviewing the conservative Republican senator Bob Dole. Here was a spectrum of opinion that went from far-right to moderately far-right. It would be interesting to see how the three of them would use the program as a vehicle for the political pluralism and diversity that is said to characterize our political system and our media. A few years earlier I had been a guest on "Crossfire" when Robert Novak was serving as host. He never let me finish a sentence in what turned out to be a half-hour screaming match. I suspected that Evans and Novak would let Dole finish *his* sentences, which was enough reason for me to flip the dial and move on.

An hour later CNN offered a program called "Newsmaker Saturday." The guests were Zbigniew Brzezinski, former national security advisor and full-time Cold War Russophobe, and Jeane Kirkpatrick, full-time apologist for U.S. interventionism in the Third World and lover of right-wing dictatorships and their benign authoritarian torturers. Kirkpatrick used to tell us about how communist governments would never give up their monopoly on power because they were too power hungry and too brutally totalitarian. After a succession of communist governments in Eastern Europe gave up their power with only feeble gestures of resistance, she stopped pushing that line. But she was still busy defending the violent U.S.-sponsored repression in El Salvador. Brzezinski and Kirkpatrick were going to talk about:

"Internal Soviet Violence: What Does It Mean?" I decided not to risk exposure to either of them.

Getting on in the day, CBS was offering a program called "Inside Washington." No guest experts were listed, just a panel of TV news analysts who were scheduled to discuss: "D.C. Mayor Marion Barry's drug arrest and ongoing civil unrest in the Soviet Union." This listing seemed to imply that there was a connection between these two subjects. So I skipped the show.

Playing against CBS—and this is what we mean by choice—was CNN's "Capital Gang." This show turned out to be a panel of news pundits who talked about "D.C. Mayor Marion Barry's arrest and internal violence in Soviet Azerbaijan." For an additional dollop of diversity, the guest was conservative Republican Orrin Hatch, whom I hadn't laid eyes on since a MacNeil-Lehrer NewsHour interview five days before. Hatch causes me to break out in a rash, so I passed.

Playing against both CBS and CNN was still more diversity: "The McLaughlin Group," an NBC program headed by a right-wing *National Review* editor named John McLaughlin. This was just one of several shows that McLaughlin presided over. It offered the usual format: three loud aggressive right-wingers (counting McLaughlin, the "moderator") would outshout two milder and polite centrists in what purported to be a political "discussion." The listed topics were—you got it: "The arrest of D.C. Mayor Marion Barry and civil war in Soviet Azerbaijan." But there was a third topic: "Bush's approval rating." I decided I would view a show about Bush's approval rating only when that rating began to drop drastically. Anyway, watching McLaughlin is a little like getting mauled in an alley.

Finally, I noticed another program listing on C-SPAN, "Journalists' Roundtable," consisting of another group of pundits who were going to talk about three topics: "Unrest in the Soviet Union, the arrest of D.C. Mayor Marion Barry, and a review of Bush's first year in office."

There you have it: the entire TV public affairs programming for January 20, 1990, in the capital of our great democracy. The only thing missing was Newt Gingrich. He arrived later and just as often. By the end of the day, I concluded that two sides of a story are not *all* sides of a story; in fact, they are sometimes not even two sides.

Not long after this, I happened to be interviewed by a Bulgarian political scientist. He was in Washington doing research on how the U.S. government worked. He remarked that America was the oldest democracy in the world and he looked forward to the day when public discourse in his own country could be as open and varied as in our country. Oh, I thought to myself, he should wish for more than that. Much more.

Meanwhile, we continue to hear that the news media are dominated by a left-liberal cabal. Some even claim that opinion in the media is far left. I would have to ask where in the mainstream media is the Left to be found? On NBC, which is owned by General Electric, one of the richest, most politically reactionary corporations in the world? On ABC, owned by Disney, another reactionary corporation? On CBS, owned by Westinghouse? On Fox, owned by billionaire Rupert Murdoch, who describes himself as a "radical conservative" and who admits he controls the political and opinion content of his newspapers and broadcast media? If these people are "left" or "liberal," then I'm the Easter Bunny.

Let's correctly label the corporate-dominated media, the big chain newspapers, and the big corporate advertisers who dominate both commercial and public media. They exercise power over the news and over publicly visible opinion; they pick the executives who hire the pundits who tell us what to think about the world. And they want us to think the same way they do. The monopoly in media ownership also brings a monopoly in mainstream media ideology.

The pundits offer little or no diversity. In knowing tones and with much heat but little light, they argue with each other over political personalities, election predictions, and trivialities. Like so many theater critics or high-flown gossips, they offer their opinions on whether the president is successfully projecting a positive image, whether this or that politico is being groomed for a leadership slot, whether Congress is in a mood to get along with the White House, and whether the CIA dropped the ball on predicting some new development. They focus on process and rarely on content.

One has to marvel at all the emphasis on style with no attention to substance, all this focus on what policy will get through with no thought about who among the public will benefit or be harmed by the policy, all this speculation about the future with no attention to present politico-economic realities. If these pundits are offering us democratic diversity, who needs totalitarian uniformity?

IS IT SPORTS OR IS IT WAR?

As presented on television, sports in America have little to do with sportsmanship and plenty to do with militarism and the national ego. Instead of bringing nations together, international sports seem to fuel that winning-is-everything mentality, a hostile rah-rah competitiveness that defeats the purpose of international games.

The link between sports and war is sometimes explicitly drawn. We might recall how militaristic hype was injected into major sporting events to bolster the Gulf War of 1991. The televised National Football League conference championship began with Army, Navy, Marine, and Air Force personnel in parade dress uniform, carrying flags down the field as the crowd chanted "USA! USA!" The 1991 Superbowl game on ABC seemed like a feature-length promo for the U.S. onslaught perpetrated against the Iraqi people, with a gigantic superpatriotic pageant, the crowd waving flags and singing patriotic songs, and a taped appearance of

President Bush and his wife. At half-time, Peter Jennings came on with an upbeat update on the destruction of Iraq.

During that time, just about every NBA basketball team, and some college teams too, had American flags sewn on their uniforms, as one announcer pointed out, "in support of our efforts in the Gulf." In a joint venture with the Department of Defense, the NFL even saw fit to sponsor a sixty-minute documentary on "Operation Desert Storm." Steve Sobol, president of NFL Films, put it this way: "I don't want to say that war is the same as football. But, the same spirit and ideology that football glorifies is also the spirit necessary for a successful military endeavor."

Team contests between the United States and the Soviet Union provided ample occasion for flag-waving and Red-bashing. When the U.S. Olympic hockey team defeated a second-string Soviet team at Lake Placid, New York, years ago, the ABC Nightline announcer crowed: "The Americans withstood an all-out Soviet assault." In an aftergame interview, the U.S. coach said he had told his players they "have something the Russians don't have — the American belief we can succeed at anything we do." Had the Soviets claimed such a faith in their own invincibility, it would have been taken as evidence of their aggrandizing intentions.

When the Soviet Union beat the USA in basketball in the 1988 Olympics, NBC treated it as the end of civilization as we know it. In postgame commentaries, NBC announcers described an American team seriously handicapped by insufficient practice time and the loss of a key player and thus unable to withstand "the Soviet onslaught." The Soviets, it seems, "never let up their attack," and were a "relentless juggernaut." A juggernaut? The impression left was that the American players were facing the Red Army rather than another basketball team. It was after this defeat that the United States decided to enter professional basketball players in the Olympics.

Telecasting of Olympic games has been marked by rah-rah chauvinism. It is one thing for American viewers to favor their own country in international athletic contests, but quite another to be urged to do so by the media. The networks project an image of U.S. athletic superiority, focusing mostly on American Olympic contestants to the neglect of those from other countries, including many who might give superior performances.

The Olympics are supposed to promote international good will and an enjoyment of the capabilities of athletes from all nations, not a shrill nationalism. ABC's coverage of the 1984 Summer Olympics was so shamelessly lopsided as to evoke an official reprimand from the normally placid International Olympic Committee. Similar complaints were registered by South Korean officials regarding NBC's coverage of the 1988 Olympics in Seoul.

The 1996 Olympics coverage was more of the same. The sports in which the USA did not compete or did not excel got little coverage. Soccer is many times more popular than any other sport throughout the world. But we saw almost none of it, because the U.S. team was not very good and got eliminated early. Volleyball is not as popular in the world, but we saw lots of it because the U.S. had a strong team. Softball is a relatively rare international sport but we saw lots of it because the Americans were winning most of the softball medals.

The camera concentrates on U.S. competitors even to the point of neglecting other nationals who finished ahead. For instance, in the kayaking competition we saw a pre-meet interview of the American Davey Hearn, we saw his wife, we even saw them getting married, and we saw him through most of the race. The only trouble is our Davey finished ninth. First place went to a Slovak, whose name I didn't quite catch because it flashed across the screen for only an instant. In another event, the U.S. entry was allotted an extensive interview — without mention of the fact that he finished sixteenth. In some instances, the medal winners were never even announced if they were not Americans.

Sometimes racism wins out over nation-state chauvinism. In the triple jump, the gold medal was won by Kenny Harrison, an American but an African American. However, TV coverage concentrated on second-place

Jonathan Edwards, a White Englishman, who happened to be a devout Christian, who talked about his gift from God to compete and how he would never compete on Sundays — until he realized he was missing out on too many opportunities, then it seems God sent him a different message. The bronze went to a Cuban whose final jump was not even shown.

And let us not forget the American fans at these games, screaming for the kill, completely immune to the spirit of international fellowship, showing no sign of hospitality (the Olympics were in Atlanta), never applauding for the foreign teams, practically snarling with rage when the Cuban women's volleyball team beat the U.S. team. The American fans roared their delight when seven-foot NBA pros pulverized a ragged team from Zaire, composed of kids who have to work for a living and who might have practiced in their spare time just a few months before.

I like sports. I just do not like the unsportsmanlike competitiveness and rabid flag-waving jingoism that comes with the coverage. It felt more like Munich 1936 than Atlanta 1996. With sports, we need to foster international friendship and the more gracious side of the human spirit. Let us have less chest-thumping and more handshaking, less emphasis on who wins and more on how the game is played. Better a family of nations than a multitude of screaming nationalistic egos.

KOZY WITH THE KLAN

The mainstream media downplay or completely ignore the many demonstrations that progressive forces have launched against war and social injustice. But not all demonstrators are slighted. Since the early 1970s, when the press first started announcing that the country was in a "conservative mood," the Ku Klux Klan has been accorded generous coverage. Lengthy and not altogether unsympathetic articles have appeared in the *New York Times*, *Washington Post*, Associated Press, *Time*, *Newsweek*, and other publications. Klan leaders, skinheads, and other hate-mongers have appeared on just about every local and national TV talk show. Indeed, the Klan and the media have often seemed entwined in a cozy embrace.

The press displays a similar partiality toward ultra-right political candidates. Nazi-Klansman David Duke received more national media running unsuccessfully for a seat in the Louisiana state legislature than did socialist Bernard Sanders running for the U.S. Congress in

Vermont and *winning*. Likewise, right-wing presidential aspirants Pat Buchanan and Ross Perot received immediate and lavish media attention upon announcing their candidacies, while the progressive Senator Tom Harkin remained unseen and largely unmentioned throughout the entire campaign.

Do we want the press to cover or ignore the Klan? The question is poorly put. We certainly want people to be informed about the menace posed by hate groups like the KKK and the American Nazi Party, but we also do not want the media to become promoters of fascists and racists. So the question is not how much coverage but what kind of coverage. Here are some specific criticisms:

1. *The press regularly fails to report the Klan's worst features.* Almost nothing is reported in depth about its racism, fascism, anticommunism, and anti-Semitism, and almost nothing about its history of violence, arson, terrorism, murder, and lynching. Some of that history is not far past: in the last fifteen years at least nine persons have died at the hands of Klan members, while scores have been harassed, intimidated, or injured.

2. *The press has lavished attention on the Klan and Nazis, thereby magnifying their visibility and exaggerating their strength and importance.* Ten demonstrators marching for some progressive cause would not win national media attention, but Klan and Nazi gatherings of that size have been treated as big news. When the Klan

held a much-publicized rally just outside Washington, D.C., in Montgomery County, Maryland, numbering all of 24 individuals in robes, 140 media people were there to transmit the event to national audiences. The *Nashville Tennessean* once ran a nine-part series on the Klan. The series mentioned that the KKK had a "dangerous potential for violence and terror," but it never elucidated the nature of that potential or mentioned specific acts. However, it did offer a generous sampling of the Klan's racist opinions. Gannet news service quickly shot the story over the wires and all three major networks reported it. As a result, the Klan's "Imperial Wizard," who liked the articles, started receiving letters from people asking how they could join. The *Tennessean* had conveniently published his address.

3. *The press downplays the anti-Klan demonstrators whose numbers are many times larger than KKK participants.* The political statement that anti-Klan demonstrators make on behalf of social justice and against racism is usually ignored by the press. The public is left to conclude that they are just hecklers spoiling for a fight. Andy Stapp, writing in *Workers World*, offers some instances of double-standard reporting:

Anti-Klan demonstrators outnumbered the fascists ten to one at a KKK rally in Connecticut, but CBS, ABC and NBC all focused their cameras on the Klan.

Fifty Klansmen parading from Selma to Montgomery
drew national attention while 500 [civil rights advo-
cates] marching against racism (67 of whom were
arrested) from Savannah to Reidsville prison the same
week were virtually censored out of the news.

Ten armed KKK terrorists rate a six-column article and a
large picture in the *New York Times*, the same newspaper which printed *not one word* about the 350,000
black and white people who demonstrated together
[for affirmative action and civil rights] in Washington,
D.C., the capital of the U.S.

4. *The press has no unkind words about how police
and government agents collaborate with the Klan and
the Nazis,* as when police attack anti-Klan protestors and
when undercover agents—who supposedly infiltrate the
KKK to keep an eye on it—end up playing key organizing roles. One investigation revealed that most of the
Klan chapters in certain parts of the South were organized and financed by the FBI. Back in November 1979,
a group of Klansmen and Nazis murdered five
Communist Workers Party leaders and wounded nine
others at an anti-Klan rally in Greensboro, N.C. The role
played by FBI and police undercover agents in organizing and arming the Greensboro terrorists remained a
story much neglected by the major news media.

The media usually label communists and socialists

as the "extreme left" and equate them with the extreme right of Nazis and Ku Kluxers—which is tantamount to equating those who oppose racism, fascism, anti-Semitism, and union-busting with those who support such things. The left "extremists," however, do not get the kind of lavish media exposure accorded the Klan. Thus, for years Charlene Mitchell and Angela Davis headed a very active multiracial organization known as the National Alliance Against Racism and Political Repression. But most people, including many on the left, never heard of the organization even though one of its leaders was a nationally known figure. Like other antiracist groups, the NAARPR suffered from a severe case of media blackout. Fighting racism is not as news-worthy as advocating and practicing racism.

Nazis and Ku Kluxers may be racist and violent but they are not anticapitalist, which might explain why the corporate press treats them so well. Indeed, throughout much of its history, the Klan functioned as a union-bust-ing organization, as did the Nazis in Germany in the early 1930s. Both the Nazi party and the Klan are explic-itly anticommunist and antisocialist. At a demonstration in Springfield, Massachusetts, the Klan distributed a leaflet denouncing the "Black Socialist Democratic People's Government" in Washington, D.C., which it claimed was plotting to overthrow "White America."

The Klan conjures up imaginary threats to explain

away real social problems, attempting to divide people along racial lines by transforming their legitimate economic grievances into a hatred of African Americans, Latinos, Asians, Jews, trade unionists, communists, welfare recipients, and advocates of affirmative action.

The media's coverage of the Klan and the far Right in general over the last twenty years has done its part to keep conservative forces in an ascendant mode. The press gives maximum exposure to the Klansmen, Nazis, skinheads, hatemongers, David Dukes, and Pat Buchanans—all of which widens the rightward range of visible discourses for the George Bushes. Of course, the media do not see it that way. They believe they just go out and get the story. Were they to join in the battle against racism, they would, by their view, be guilty of "advocacy journalism." So instead of exposing hate groups, the press gives exposure *to* hate groups. That is called "objectivity."

★★★

"INFERIOR" PEOPLE

For centuries, colonialists have justified their mistreatment of other peoples by portraying them as lacking ethical, cultural, and political development. If there is turmoil in some part of the Third World, then the trouble supposedly rests with the people themselves and not with anything the intruders are doing to them.

In 1973, when the CIA-engineered coup in Chile overthrew Salvador Allende and led to the bloody repression of the Pinochet regime, "blaming the people" became the media's favorite explanation. CBS commentator Eric Sevareid announced that the Chilean people brought it on themselves, another Latin American example of "an instability so chronic that the root causes have to lie in the nature and culture of the people." By way of explaining why Chileans would support Allende and the Popular Unity government, Barnard Collier wrote in the *New York Times*, "The Chileans do not believe in facts, numbers or statistics with the earnest faith of an English-speaking people." While talking to a correspondent who had just reported on the rebellion in Tigre, NBC's Tom Brokaw could only think of asking, "You're in London now, which is one of the most sophisticated and civilized cities in the world. Do you have much culture shock after being in that part of Africa?"

During the Cold War years, the Russians were a prime target of stereotypic pronouncements. They were described by one U.S. correspondent as "unsmiling," "rude," and "unable to look you in the eye." A former *Washington Post* reporter, appearing on ABC's "20/20" program, declared that "the Russians have a great urge for order. It is part of their personality." To which host Barbara Walters responded that the Russian people lacked "a sense of responsibility because they are told what to do and when to do it." In 1991, at a time of dramatic transition within the Soviet Union, the *New York Times* noted that Russian free-market advocates "faced the mammoth task of civilizing their country."

The Arabs are another people who are treated to a superabundance of negative stereotypes. A CBS correspondent ended his report on the Middle East by saying, "But, of course, sound argument has not always dictated Arab behavior." *New York Times* columnist Flora Lewis saw "the Islamic mind" as unable to employ "step-by-step thinking." Had such an assertion been applied to "the Christian mind" or "the Hebrew mind," the *Times* likely would have rejected it as nonsensical and bigoted, and rightly so.

The 1990–91 Gulf War waged by the United States against Iraq brought a wave of anti-Arab stereotypes. (Iraq was an Arab nation but so were six of the nations allied with Washington.) *Newsday* referred to "the treacherous standards of Arab politics." Judith Miller in the *New York Times* claimed that the Gulf Cooperation Council, in "typical Arab style" made a "veiled reference" to the presence of U.S. forces in the Gulf. Miller would never describe an Israeli leader as making a veiled reference in "typical Jewish style." Nor would that be a proper or correct usage.

U.S. News and World Report quoted "Middle East specialist" Judith Kipper on the devious nature of the "Arab mind": "*We* go in a straight line; *they* zig-zag. They say one thing in the morning, another thing at night and really mean a third thing." *New Republic* editor Martin Peretz warned us, "Nonviolence is foreign to the political culture of Arabs generally and of the Palestinians particularly." *New York Times* columnist A. M. Rosenthal listed Iranians as Arabs, leaving his readers to remind themselves that Iranians are in fact Persians. That they all live in the Middle East is no reason to lump Arabs and Persians together, no more than we would think of the French as being German because they both live in Europe.

One of the media's favorite Middle East "experts," Fouad Ajami (praised by columnist William Safire "for the amazing way he reads the Arab mind") described Iraq as "a brittle land . . . with little claim to culture and books and grand ideas." In fact, Iraq was the cradle of a long and fertile civilization. And before it was destroyed by American bombs, Baghdad was a major center of literature, art, and architecture.

NPR's Susan Stamberg interviewing two Arab intellectuals, asked them to comment on an association in her mind: "Arabs and death." They patiently explained that like everyone else, Arabs preferred life over death for themselves and their loved ones. Then she gave them another association: "Arabs and violence." Stamberg resides in the United States, a country with one of the highest violent crime rates in the world, a country that spends $275 billion yearly on the military and supports violent repression through much of the Third World, and which at that very moment was waging a murderous war against a vastly smaller and weaker Arab nation—and she was wondering why Arabs were so violent.

The U.S. media regularly treat various ethnic groups in a derogatory way. Thus the news media have little positive to say about the struggles of African Americans, Native Americans, and others for jobs, decent housing, safe neighborhoods, and viable political organizations. Moreover, the efforts of people of color to gain recognition in art, literature, entertainment, music, sports, religion, labor, and education have earned relatively scant notice in the corporate-owned white media.

African Americans *are* generously overrepresented in the news when there is bad news to report. Polling statistics in *USA Today* show that only 15 percent of U.S. drug users are African American, but data from the Black Entertainment Network indicate that 50 percent of network news stories on drugs focus on African Americans.

As media commentators, African Americans remain drastically underrepresented. Mayor Richard Hatcher of Gary, Indiana, noted, "About the only time you really see blacks giving their opinions, or given any serious space, is when it relates to minorities or civil rights. That seems to be the only time when the media feel we are competent enough to express opinions." Even in that area, blacks who express ideas on race that run counter to the predominant ideological mode are likely to be subjected to attack. Reputable African American scholars and educators have tried to move away from a Eurocentric approach to history and set the record straight with university curricula that treat the often neglected African and African American experience. But these efforts have been vehemently denounced by the white media as "bad history" and "ethnic cheerleading."

In contrast, conservative African American writers and academics, like Thomas Sowell and Shelby Steele, who serve as cheerleaders for the status quo, are given generous exposure as they denounce affirmative action and other federal programs designed to help ethnic minorities, and as they praise the established power structure and downplay the effects of racism in the United States. Unfortunately, but not surprisingly, Eurocentric racism is alive and well in the corporate-owned media.

PICTURES IN OUR HEADS

Even if supposedly not political in intent, the multibillion-dollar film and television industries are political in impact, discouraging critical perceptions of our social order, while planting pictures in our heads that support U.S. militarism, armed intervention abroad, phobic anti-communism, authoritarian violence, vigilantism, consumer acquisitiveness, racial and sexual stereotypes, and anti-working-class attitudes.

Remarking on the prevalence of media-induced stereotypes of African Americans, Ellen Holly put it well:

> Again and again, I have seen Black actors turned down for parts because they were told that they did not look the way a Black person should or sound the way a Black person should. What is this business of "should"? What kind of box are we being put into? I have seen Black writers told that the

Black characters they put down on a page were not believable because they were too intelligent (*Black Scholar* Jan./Feb. 1979).

Studies show that women too, are put into a box, portrayed mostly in subsidiary roles and depicted as less capable, effective, or interesting than the more numerous white male principals. To be sure, things have changed somewhat. Women can now be seen playing lawyers, judges, cops, executives, professionals, and sometimes even workers, but the questions of gender equality and the fight for feminist values are seldom joined. Likewise, the struggles of sleep-starved, underpaid single mothers trying to raise their children and survive in an inhospitable environment are not usually considered an appropriate theme for prime-time television or Hollywood.

Working people of both genders and whatever ethnic background are still underrepresented in the media, usually consigned to playing minor walk-on roles as waiters, service people, gas station attendants, and the like in an affluent, upper-middle-class, media-created world. Blue-collar people are portrayed as emotional, visceral, simple-hearted, simple-minded, and incapable of leadership or collective action against the injustices they face in their workplace and community. Their unions are depicted as doing more harm than good. Given the hostility that network and studio bosses have manifested toward organized labor in the entertainment industry, it is small wonder that labor unions are almost always portrayed, if at all, in an unsympathetic light.

Generally speaking, whether it is a movie about factory workers, cops, and crime, or the invasion of galactic monsters, it is individual heroics rather than collective action that save the day. Solutions and victories are never won by ordinary good people, organizing and struggling for mutual betterment, but by the hero in self-willed combat, defying the odds and sometimes even the authorities to vanquish the menace and let justice triumph.

In great supply as heroes are the purveyors of violence and macho toughness: the military man, cop, counterinsurgency agent, spy-catcher, private investigator, and adventurer, with their helicopter gunships, screeching car chases, and endless shoot-'em-ups and punch-'em-outs, to which today we can add the eerie wonders of computerized high-tech weaponry. Check the movie ads in your newspaper for the number of weapons displayed. Flip your TV dial during prime time and count the number of guns or fistfights or other acts of violence and aggression (not to mention the verbal aggressions and put-downs that are the stock-in-trade of the sitcoms).

Iconoclastic opinions and images get through now and then. Liberal and even strongly progressive themes can be found in an occasional movie or television episode. Underdog and dissident voices are heard, but only on the rarest occasions.

In modern mass society, people rely to a great extent upon distant image-makers for their cues about the wider world and even about their own immediate experience. Our notion of what a politician, a corporate executive, a farmer, an African, or a Mexican American are supposed to be like; our view of what rural or inner-city life should be; our anticipations about romantic experience and sexual attractiveness, crime and foreign enemies, dictators and revolutionaries, bureaucrats and protestors, police and prostitutes, workers and communists—all are heavily colored by our exposure to movies and TV shows.

Many of us have never met an Arab, but few of us lack some picture in our minds of what an Arab is supposed to be like. If drawn largely from the mass media, this image will be a stereotype, and most likely a defamatory one. As Walter Lippmann noted almost seventy years ago in his book *Public Opinion*, stereotypic thinking "precedes reason" and "as a form of perception [it] imposes a certain character on the data of our senses." When we respond to a real-life situation with the exclamation, "Just like in the movies!" we are expressing our recognition and even satisfaction that our media-created mental frames find corroboration in the actual world.

The media images in our heads influence how we appraise a host of social realities, including U.S. domestic and foreign policies. If we have "learned" from motion pictures and television series that our nation is forever threatened by hostile alien forces, then we are apt to support increased military spending and warlike interventions. If we have "learned" that inner-city denizens are violent criminals and welfare chiselers, then we are more apt to support authoritarian police measures and cuts in human services to the inner city.

Audiences usually do some perceptual editing. They frequently project something of their own viewpoint upon what they see. But this editing itself is partly conditioned by the previously internalized images fed to us by the same media we are now viewing. In other words, rather than being rationally critical of the images and ideologies of the entertainment media, our minds — after prolonged exposure to earlier programs and films — sometimes become active accomplices in our own indoctrination.

Children believe that what they are seeing on television and in the movies is real; they have no innate capacity to distinguish between real and unreal images. Only as they grow older, after repeated assurances from their elders, do they begin to understand that the stories and characters on the big and little screens do not exist in real life. In other words, their ability to reject media images as unreal has to be learned.

The problem does not end there. Even as adults,

when we consciously know that a particular media offering is fictional, we still absorb impressions that lead to beliefs about the real world. When drawing upon images in our heads, we do not keep our store of media imagery distinct and separate from our store of real-world imagery.

The most pervasive effect of television — aside from its content — may be its very existence, its readily available, commanding, and often addictive presence in our homes, its ability to reduce hundreds of millions of citizens to passive spectators for major portions of their waking hours. Television minimizes interactions between persons within families and communities. One writer I know only half-jokingly claims, "I watch television as a way of getting to know my husband and children." Another associate, who spent years in Western agrarian regions, relates how a farmer once told her: "Folks used to get together a lot. Now with television, we see less of each other."

The more time people spend watching television and movies, the more their impressions of the world seem to resemble those of the media. Studies show that heavy television users, having been fed abundant helpings of crime and violence, are more likely to overestimate the amount of crime and violence that exists in society. They are also more apt to overestimate the number of police in the United States, since they see so many on TV.

It is not just a matter of the entertainment industry giving the people what they want; it plays an active role in creating those wants. Those who produce images for mass consumption exercise an enormous power, but they are not entirely free from public pressure. The viewing audience is sometimes more than just a passive victim. There are occasions when popular agitation, advances in democratic consciousness, and changes in public taste and educational levels have forced the media to modify or discard the images they feed us. The public has to keep fighting back. We got rid of Amos 'n' Andy and Sambo; we can get rid of Dirty Harry and Rambo along with other representations of mindless violence and militarism.

More important than eliminating the bad shows is demanding better ones for our children and ourselves. Better entertainment that is not only intelligent and socially significant but also capable of attracting large audiences usually gets poorly distributed and modestly advertised, if at all.

The entertainment media become a problem when they become a way of life, preempting our experience and taking over our brains, providing us with a prefabricated understanding of what the world is supposed to be. This it does for too many people. A better awareness of how we are manipulated by the make-believe media might cause us to waste fewer precious hours in front of the big and little screens and allow us more time for reading, conversing, relating to our friends and families, crit-icizing social injustice, and becoming active citizens of our society and more effective agents of our own lives.

CONCLUSION

★ ★ ★

WHAT IS TO BE DONE (FOR STARTERS)?

It should be no mystery what needs to be done to improve our economy and the life conditions of our people.

The military spending binge is the major cause of the nation's $5 trillion national debt, runaway deficits, decaying infrastructure, and high taxes. It has transformed the United States from the world's biggest lender into the world's biggest spender and debtor. To save $2 trillion over the next decade, we should cut the bloated "defense" budget by two-thirds.

Eliminate the expensive nuclear missile systems designed to fight a total war against a superpower that no longer exists. Shut down almost all of the hundreds of U.S. military bases abroad and stop playing the self-appointed global guardian who monitors everyone else's behavior on behalf of the free market.

Stop all nuclear tests, including underground ones, and support a nuclear-free world. End the manned space program, a $30 billion boondoggle whose major contribution has been to wreak destruction upon the ozone layer.

Government should eliminate the multibillion-dollar welfare handouts to rich corporations and agribusiness. Let them try living up to their free-market rhetoric. The monies saved from these cuts could be used to employ millions of people to build affordable housing, schools, and mass transit; rebuild our parks, towns, cities, and a crumbling infrastructure; reclaim the environment; and provide services for the aged, the infirm, and the rest of us, including a single-payer health care system.

Let us end U.S.-sponsored counterinsurgency wars against the poor of the world. The billions of our tax dollars given to corrupt regimes, with their death squads and torturers engaged in every conceivable human rights violation, could be better spent on human services at home.

In addition, Congress should abolish the CIA and drastically cut the budget of other intelligence agencies. Their mandates should be limited to intelligence gathering. Prohibit their violent covert actions within Third World nations and social movements. Expose and end their domestic counterinsurgency programs that attempt to disrupt and demoralize potentially rebellious communities and dissident organizations.

The Freedom of Information Act should be enforced instead of undermined by those who say they have nothing to hide, then try to hide almost everything they do.

We need to curb the moneyed interests and lobbyists. All candidates, including minor-party ones, should be provided with public campaign financing. The campaigns themselves should be limited in duration and all candidates should be accorded free access to the major media in the weeks before the election.

The airwaves are the property of the people of the United States. As part of their public-service licensing requirements, television and radio stations should be required to give — free of charge — equal public air time to *all* political viewpoints, including radical ones. Only then can the present globalistic, free-market orthodoxy be challenged before mass audiences.

The states should institute proportional representation so that every vote will count and voters will have a wider and more democratic choice of parties, which in turn, as other countries have shown, leads to a higher level of voter participation. Also needed is a standard federal electoral law allowing easy ballot access for third parties and independents, and imposing stricter monitoring of vote tabulations.

Government could dramatically lower the deficit by reintroducing the progressive income tax for rich individuals and corporations — without the many loopholes and deductions that still exist, and expand rather than cut the capital gains tax on big investors.

Strengthen the inheritance tax. At the same time,

give tax relief to the working poor and other low-income employees. Reduce the regressive Social Security tax; it produces a yearly $50 billion surplus that is shifted into the general budget. Or increase Social Security payments to low-income elderly so that the surplus is spent in a way it was intended.

Abolish antilabor laws that make it so difficult for people to organize unions. Penalize employers with heavy fines who refuse to negotiate a contract after certification has been won. Repeal the restrictive "right to work" and "open shop" laws that undermine collective bargaining. Pass a law prohibiting the hiring of scab (permanent replacement) workers during a strike.

We need more law and order; that is, more protection for women and children who suffer widespread violence and abuse, more protection for consumers and workers, and for abortion clinics, and ethnic groups, immigrants, gays, and others who have been targeted by hate groups.

Corporate heads who repeatedly violate the law, causing serious harm to human life and the environment, and who cheat the government and the public of millions of dollars with fraudulent contracts, should be sent to jail instead of given light fines.

Withdraw from NAFTA and GATT, international agreements that circumvent popular sovereignty, endow multinational corporatism with still greater privileges, and cripple protections for labor, consumers, independent producers, and the environment.

Encourage organic commercial farming and expeditiously phase out the use of pesticides, chemical fertilizers, and livestock hormones. Initiate a long overdue crash program to develop thermal, hydro, tidal, and solar energy sources.

Develop high-speed, mass-transit, magnetic monorail systems within and between cities for safe, swift, economical transportation, and electric and solar-powered vehicles to minimize the disastrous ecological effects of fossil fuels.

In sum, public policy should be directed to the needs of the many rather than the greed of the few. The problem we face is that the ruling interests are profoundly committed to a vision of the world that is ruthlessly exploitative, hegemonic, self-serving, and ecologically unsustainable. Our only choice is to expose and oppose them with all our concerted effort.

★ ★ ★

WE *MUST* FIGHT CITY HALL

Many people are of the opinion that it is futile to try to
effect meaningful political change, a view summed up in
the old adage, "You can't fight City Hall." We are
advised not to expect government to respond to our
demands. As conservatives and anarchists alike would
say, government cannot solve problems, government *is*
the problem. Certainly, in many areas of public life, government is a negative force, an instrument of coercive
power that helps to intensify rather than mitigate the
inequities suffered by millions of people at home and
abroad. Government in the hands of the privileged and
powerful will advance the interests of the privileged and
powerful—unless democratic forces can mobilize a
countervailing power. And that is the question.

Who are the privileged and powerful? Those who
own the banks, corporations, factories, mines, news and
entertainment industries, and agribusiness firms of this
country are what is meant by the "owning class" or the

"rich." The "ruling elites" or "ruling class" are the politically active portion of the owning class. They and their faithful acolytes and scribes compose the Business Roundtable, the Business Council, the Trilateral Commission, and the Council on Foreign Relations, organizations started by the Rockefellers, Mellons, Morgans, and other economic royalists. From their ranks are recruited the secretaries of State, Defense, and Treasury, national security advisors and CIA directors, and, indeed, U.S. senators, presidents, and vice presidents. For the very top positions of state, the ruling class is largely self-recruiting.

The privileged and the powerful arguably are America's most costly welfare class. Each year, from local, state, and federal governments, they receive billions and billions of dollars in subsidies and grants, supports and interest-free loans, tax credits and tax deductions. Cities across the nation are closing hospitals and libraries, clinics and schools, while they build privatized prisons and huge sports arenas at great cost to taxpayers and great profit to already filthy rich private owners.

That is how the privileged and powerful operate. They denounce government handouts to the poor and needy, while they themselves feed shamelessly at the public trough. They denounce government regulations, then rig the regulations to suit their own interests as with the Omnibus Communications Act, which paved the way for still more concentrated and corporatized broadcast media by allowing large media interests to buy up small ones, without regard for considerations of diversity.

A political system in which wealth and class play such a dominant role seems to leave little opportunity for progressive betterment. Popular sentiment is often denied a hearing. People are repeatedly deceived or distracted with a never-ending panorama of pop culture and media puffery. Dissidents are harassed, suppressed, and sometimes even assassinated. In time, people lapse into cynicism and sour resignation. In such a situation, a demoralized passivity assumes the guise of a false consensus.

Certainly, some commentators treat political dis-couragement and quietude as symptomatic of content-ment, arguing that we are too happy with our abundance and freedom to engage in political struggle. Right-wing columnist George Will writes, "Low [voter] turnouts often are signs of social health. Low political energy can be a consequence of consensus about basics" (*Washington Post*, Sept. 9, 1991). Since turnout is lowest among the low-income poor and the unemployed, the overworked and underpaid, the disadvantaged and the disabled, lowest in crime-ridden and drug-besieged communities, presum-ably they must be the most contented and socially healthy of all. In fact, the evidence says otherwise.

Despite the powerful array of forces against them,

many people still organize, protest, and resist — sometimes with an impressive measure of success. In recent decades we have witnessed a number of powerful democratic movements: the civil rights protests to enfranchise African Americans in the South and end lynch-mob rule and segregation, the civil liberties struggle against McCarthyism and government harassment of dissidents, the movement to end the Vietnam war, the anti-imperialist solidarity for El Salvador and Nicaragua, the attempts to build alternative educational and informational institutions, the movement for a nuclear freeze and an end to the arms race, and the struggles for women's rights, gay rights, and environmentalism.

During those same years, we have seen long and bitter labor struggles valiantly fought by coal miners, steel workers, farm laborers, airline employees, newspaper staffs, bus drivers, teachers, university staff, health industry employees, and others. While probably none of these mass movements and labor struggles has met with unqualified success, all have made a difference. All have had an impact in limiting how far the rich and powerful can go in advancing their otherwise uncompromising global pursuit of maximum profit and endless privilege.

The conventional view is that power is antithetical to freedom, a threat to it. This can be true of *state* power and other forms of institutionalized authority. However, *popular* power and freedom are not antithetical but complementary: if you do not have the power to limit the abuses of wealth and position, you do not have much freedom. In order to wrest democratic gains from entrenched interests, we the people must mobilize a countervailing power. "The concessions of the privileged to the unprivileged," wrote John Stuart Mill in 1869, "are so seldom brought about by any better motive than the power of the unprivileged to extort them. . . ."

The goal of popular action is not only to limit or rebuff state power but to make it work for democratic ends as opposed to plutocratic ends. Rather than saying "you cannot fight city hall," we might better say that we cannot afford not to. It is often frustrating and sometimes dangerous to challenge those who own and control the land, labor, capital, and technology of society. But, in the long run, it is even more dangerous not to do so.

As history shows, people frequently endeavor to resist the disadvantages imposed upon them by unjust socio-economic conditions. They may be propelled by a vision of a better life for all, or by the imperatives of a particular issue, or by the necessities of their own material conditions. Inequities and iniquities can become so oppressive that submission no longer guarantees survival and the people have nothing to lose in resisting. This is not to say they will always rebel against oppression, but the right combination of anger, hope, and organization sometimes can galvanize them to perform remarkable deeds.

Regarding their own interests, the worst thing people can do is to do nothing, to lapse into political quietism. In 1983, the Reagan administration's welfare chief, Linda McMahon, justified the savage cuts in human services imposed on the poorest and politically weakest element of the population by noting that their effects must have been tolerable because "We're not seeing riots. We're not seeing people rushing the doors of Congress and the White House" (*Washington Post*, Feb. 17, 1983). The image of penniless subsistence workers hopping jets to storm the capital is almost amusing. Not so the idea that the government can do what it likes to the most vulnerable among us as long as they don't take to the streets and inconvenience the rulers.

Popular passivity is the goal of all rulers who seek to preserve their entrenched privileges against the claims of the public. It is what they usually mean by "stability" and "order." The real name of their system is plutocracy, rule by the wealthy few, the very opposite of democracy. In the interest of liberty and social justice, it should be hated and fought, resisted and replaced with a system of communal ownership and rigorous democratic protections for public and private well-being.

ABOUT THE AUTHOR

MICHAEL PARENTI is considered one of the nation's leading progressive thinkers. He received his Ph.D. in political science from Yale University in 1962, and has taught at a number of colleges and universities. His writings have been featured in scholarly journals, popular periodicals, and newspapers, and articles and books of his have been translated into Spanish, Chinese, Japanese, German, Polish, Portuguese, and Turkish.

Dr. Parenti has lectured throughout North America and in Europe on college campuses and before religious, labor, community, peace, and public interest groups. He has appeared on radio and television talk shows to discuss current issues or ideas from his published works. Tapes of his talks have played on numerous radio stations to enthusiastic audiences. Audio- and videotapes of his appearances are sold on a not-for-profit basis. For a listing, contact People's Video, P.O. Box 99514, Seattle WA 98199; tel. 1-800-823-4507. Dr. Parenti lives in Berkeley, California.

CITY LIGHTS PUBLICATIONS